AWAY IN A MANGER

Away in a Manger

Resources for Advent–Christmas Preaching and Worship

Scott R. Murray

Carl Roth

Janet Muth

CONCORDIA PUBLISHING HOUSE · SAINT LOUIS

Unless otherwise noted, Scripture quotations are from the Holy Bible, English Standard Version®. Copyright © 2001 by Crossway Bibles, a publishing ministry of Good News Publishers, Wheaton, Illinois. Used by permission. All rights reserved.

Scripture quotations marked NIV are taken from the HOLY BIBLE, NEW INTERNATIONAL VERSION®. NIV®. Copyright © 1973, 1978, 1984 by International Bible Society. Used by permission of Zondervan Publishing House. All rights reserved.

Hymn texts are from *Lutheran Service Book*, copyright © 2006 Concordia Publishing House.

Some prayers taken from *Lutheran Service Book: Altar Book*, copyright © 2006 Concordia Publishing House.

Quotations marked *Luther's Small Catechism* are from *Luther's Small Catechism with Explanation*, copyright © 1986, 1991 Concordia Publishing House.

Quotations marked Luther's Works or AE are from vol. 16 of *Luther's Works*, American Edition, edited by Jaroslav Pelikan and Hilton Oswald, copyright © 1969 Concordia Publishing House; from vol. 26 of *Luther's Works*, American Edition, edited by Jaroslav Pelikan and Walter A. Hansen, copyright © 1963 Concordia Publishing House; from vol. 31 of *Luther's Works*, American Edition, edited by Harold J. Grimm, copyright © 1957 Augsburg Fortress Press; and from vol. 52 of *Luther's Works*, American Edition, edited by Hans J. Hillerbrand, copyright © 1974 Augsburg Fortress Press.

The SymbolGREEK II and HEBRAICAII fonts used to print this work are available from Linguist's Software, Inc., PO Box 580, Edmonds, WA 98020-0580, USA; telephone (425) 775-1130; www.linguistsoftware.com.

Manufactured in the United States of America

Library of Congress Cataloging-in-Publication Data

Away in a manger : resources for Advent-Christmas preaching and worship / Scott R. Murray . . . [et al].

p. cm.

ISBN 978-0-7586-1448-3

1. Advent sermons. 2. Advent sermons—Outlines, syllabi, etc. 3. Christmas sermons. 4. Christmas sermons—Outlines, syllabi, etc. 5. Worship programs. I. Murray, Scott R. II. Title.

BV4254.5.A93   2008

263'.91—dc22

2008012081

1 2 3 4 5 6 7 8 9 10   17 16 15 14 13 12 11 10 09 08

Contents

PREFACE

The Christmas cradle hymn "Away in a Manger" (*Lutheran Service Book*, 364) is a perennial favorite of children and adults. Although pastors and musicians might quibble with the thinness of the hymn's theology, it can be used to good effect as a lead-in to the deeper theology of the Second Article of the Apostles' Creed, especially as explained by Martin Luther in his Small Catechism. The work of leading the people to peer into the manger and see their Lord begins with the road map of the Old Testament. Lutherans really believe that the Old Testament revelation testifies of Christ (John 5:39)—and nowhere more clearly than in the prophecy of Isaiah. If we take seriously that the Old Testament is the manger in which the Lord lies, then it is profitable to focus on the appointed Advent texts from Isaiah included in Series A of the lectionary for *Lutheran Service Book*. Thus we have paired the tender cradle hymn with the sublime and majestic words of the fifth evangelist and connected them both with Luther's explanation of the Second Article of the Apostles' Creed.

The theological rationale for the season of Advent includes speaking of the "comings" of the Messiah among His people: first, the promised coming in the flesh; second, the promised coming in judgment; and third, the constant gracious coming by Word and Sacraments. The so-called "third coming" of Christ in Word and Sacraments is the coming between the comings. Each advent is intimately related. The first and third advents are inseparable, and both prepare for and are interpreted in view of the second advent.

"Away in a Manger" often provides the "hook" on which to hang larger and deeper theological interpretations of the incarnation and nativity of our Lord Jesus Christ (both in sermons and liturgical resources). The explanation of the Second Article of the Apostles' Creed from Luther, well-known to many parishioners, will serve the same function, as well as deepening the themes only hinted at in the hymn. Here the exploration of these doctrines—both in a childlike and a mature context—can stand together in a coherent whole and become, to misquote Gregory the Great, the stream across which elephants swim and lambs walk.

INTRODUCTION

Away in a manger, no crib for a bed,
The little Lord Jesus laid down His sweet head.
The stars in the sky looked down where He lay,
The little Lord Jesus asleep on the hay.
(Lutheran Service Book, 364:1)

Jesus Christ came once in lowliness, and He will come again in glory. Between these events, He continues to come to us in the cradle of Scripture through the Word and Sacraments. And as quaint as the hymn's confirmation of Christ's first arrival as the one "asleep on the hay" and His second arrival to "take us to heaven" may be, we should point the people of God to the coming of the Lord in the tangible means of Word, water, bread, and wine. In *Away in a Manger*, we have changed the order of the lessons as found in *Lutheran Service Book: Lectionary, Series A* to accommodate a Second Article schema.

The cattle are lowing, the baby awakes,
But little Lord Jesus, no crying He makes.
I love Thee, Lord Jesus! Look down from the sky,
And stay by my cradle till morning is nigh.
(Lutheran Service Book, 364:2)

Advent opens with a somber pitch as we experience the shadow of revelation still to be fulfilled. The season before us brings into view the big picture of both the first and second comings of Christ. Yet we interpret the second coming through the first (one can see this approach developed in more detail in the articles titled "Messianic Mountaintops" by Martin Naumann in *The Springfielder* 39:2 [1975]: 5–72). In the season of Advent, we prepare for Christ's second coming on the Last Day, for one cannot prepare for a coming that has already occurred. Also, if we inappropriately prepare for Christ's first advent as the Babe in Bethlehem, then we miss His coming in Word and Sacraments or the appropriate ongoing preparation for His coming on the Last Day.

Consider also the third and fourth paragraphs of Luther's explanation to the Second Article of the Apostles' Creed in the Small Catechism.

Be near me, Lord Jesus; I ask Thee to stay
Close by me forever and love me, I pray.
Bless all the dear children in Thy tender care,
And take us to heaven to live with Thee there.
(Lutheran Service Book, 364:3)

The Church is bracketed between "comings." But she is not abandoned by Christ Jesus (Acts 1:1–2). The Old Testament speaks of the Messiah as the "coming One." How seriously do we take the promise that Christ is always coming among us? We have a God who is present, not absent. The preaching of Law and Gospel and the proper administration of the Sacraments reveal the Church, the place where the tabernacle of God is being built in those called by the One who is the living temple. It is the site of Christ's ongoing advent among His people.

Midweek 1

CHRIST'S FIRST COMING: WHO LIES IN THE MANGER?

ISAIAH 11:1–10

GOAL

That hearers would believe that in the first coming of our Lord Jesus Christ everything is changed.

TEXTUAL NOTES

See Luther's commentary, AE 16:117–25.

Isaiah 11:1–2

Waw connects that which follows it to that which precedes it. The entire section is well demarcated by the repetition in 11:10 of "root of Jesse." The preceding section (10:33–34) speaks of the judgment of God against Assyria using the illustration of the deforestation caused by enemy armies. Forests of stumps are a powerful image. Externally, all is devastation, yet the root can bring forth fruitfulness. Appearances can be deceiving. The monarchy of Judah has been cut off, but the Lord has founded the royal house (2 Samuel 7) and preserves it. "And the surviving remnant of the house of Judah shall again take root downward and bear fruit upward" (2 Kings 19:30; Isaiah 37:31). The root (*pl.*) is an intricately intertwined support from the Lord that will give rise to the fruitfulness of the royal house in the messianic shoot. גֶּזַע ("stock or stem") appears only three times in the Masoretic Text, two times in Isaiah (11:1; 40:24). Jesse is the nonroyal father of the first king from Judah, David. The name of Jesse emphasizes the deeply rooted plans of God for the messianic house. It also is a reminder of the humble sources of that house. Jesse's humble house was a gracious choice. Isaiah had already proclaimed the fall of the Davidic house (7:17), and its revival is a further fulfillment of the promise of God and all the more glorious because of its external implausibility. A shoot (נֵצֶר) requires careful tending because it is a tender growth. The Lord Himself cares for this shoot; therefore it will be fruitful. God assures the fruitfulness of the Messiah by endowing Him with "the Spirit without measure" (John 3:34). The Messiah possesses all the endowments missing from the actual incumbents of the throne of Judah. The lowly Messiah has all the gifts for salvation that men could never have offered. The Spirit of Yahweh is the fullness of the Godhead dwelling bodily in this one Man (Colossians 1:19; 2:9). The triple dyad that follows gives the results of the incarnation for the people of God. They will be well ruled, unlike their experiences under previous royal administrations.

Isaiah 11:3–5

The Messiah's unique position enables Him to see what cannot be seen; thus His judgment strikes right to the heart of our needs. He is unimpressed by what impresses human reason and judgment. His own ministry is characterized by refusing to submit to these external and legalistic standards. He is the ultimate theologian of the cross, who "calls the thing what it actually is" (AE 31:53), no matter how it looks. The apparent weakness of His people does not lead Him to abandon them, since He will delight in the fear of the Lord. The Lord speaks them both dead and alive with the breath of His mouth. "This is the same spoken Word, and it has power both to save and to destroy. It saves the godly, that is, those who believe and make no claims for themselves, but it destroys the ungodly, that is, those who are proud in their own wisdom and righteousness. But it smites and brings to naught earthly and ungodly men, toward repentance and toward conversion and toward constant enlargement of His reign" (AE 16:121–22). This King will be prepared to use the panoply of His power on behalf of those who need His support. His righteousness and faithfulness will be used to act for others.

Isaiah 11:6–7

Human government will not only be eclipsed by the messianic administration, but also nature itself will undergo a renovation. This is indicative of the complete and far-reaching salvation worked by the arm of the Lord. What had faltered at the fall when "thorns infest the ground" (*Lutheran Service Book*, 387:3) would now be restored completely to its pristine harmony. The creatures that once would have devoured one another now live in harmony. The leadership of a Child caps all of this, though such creatures would typically endanger a child. קָטֹן connotes smallness, even insignificance. Leadership in the hands of a child is usually considered problematic, even evil. Yet despite this "insignificance," the Child, the Messiah, is the sovereign of these enemies of the fallen creation. His presence enables them to sojourn in safety (גּוּר). In the literary structure, the child is in the midst of a wild kingdom, at the center of untamed danger. "In innocence, simplicity, and faith lie the salvation of a globe grown old in sophistication, cynicism, and violence" (John Oswalt, *The Book of Isaiah: Chapters 1–39*, New International Commentary on the Old Testament [Grand Rapids: Eerdmans, 1986], 284).

Isaiah 11:8–10

The ancient enemy is overcome, so that the Child makes sport (שָׁעַע, "to engage in delightful play") of the most deadly serpent. "All who are in Christ are called children, and they enjoy dealing with devils. This, then, is the fruit of the Word, to turn men from every error and tyranny. The little boy pulls the snakes out with his hand, that is, the preacher by means of the spoken Word casts out the devils because the Holy Spirit is present" (AE 16:123). The expectation of the Church is to do greater things than these (John 1:50). Where the Lord can control the serpent's power, we, too, can handle the snakes (Mark 16:18). It becomes child's play when the Child defeats the ancient enemy. Although we do not know which poisonous serpents are being identified, the image makes the skin crawl, yet that revulsion indicates the shocking nature of the reversal it represents.

The "holy mountain" is none other than Mount Zion (Psalm 27:4; 36:8–9; 65:4), to which all people are returned by the ministry of the Child who plays around the hole of the serpent. The era of death is brought to its close by the arrival of the One who, despite apparent weakness, puts death to death. In the Messiah, the creatures that represented the constant stalk of death now are incapable of bringing harm. He who brings this salvation is the One whose knowledge is both sought and believed. The Church exists to know nothing but this knowledge, which consists of the Child who can make sport of the ancient enemy. This knowledge (דֵּעָה) is taught by the prophets to the shepherds of the people (Jeremiah 3:15), who in turn will lead the people by this knowledge (Psalm 73:10–11).

The section is brought to its literary and theological conclusion by the *inclusio* in v. 10. The sign may be as large as a sail (Ezekiel 27:7). "The nations" would include the Gentiles who are gathered to the sign of the Christ at Zion. Isaiah looks through this whole work of the Child to see the consummation of the age at which glory, now hidden, shall be revealed.

Sermon Outline

Introduction

Watch a sleeping newborn. The calm, deep breathing reveals a quiet and peaceful heart. This baby will have plenty of time to discover the trouble of this world, but for now there is no trouble, provided the child is loved and cared for well. As we look on a resting infant, the child's face often reflects the mother and father. The composed features of young children may tell us whom they favor. My two girls were blessed to receive the features of their mother.

Jesus had the features of His mother, Mary. Yet this does not tell us who He is. Jesus' physical appearance tells us only of His human heritage through David, though this is extremely important. Only God could tell us who the Child Jesus is. Our theme hymn states, "The little Lord Jesus laid down His sweet head" (*Lutheran Service Book*, 364:1). Dear God, tell us, who sleeps in the manger? What Child is this?

I.   True God, begotten of the Father from eternity (Romans 1:4)
     A.   He will judge with righteousness
     B.   He will be faithful
         1.   To His Father
         2.   To us and to our need

II.   True man, born of the Virgin Mary
     A.   Son of David (Romans 1:3)
         1.   Root and stump
         2.   Human glory cut down
     B.   Divine gifts conveyed to Him by reason
        of the personal union
         1.   Wisdom and understanding
         2.   Counsel and might
         3.   Knowledge and the fear of the Lord
     C.   The Child puts His hand in the hole of the viper
         1.   The Child crushes the serpent

2. The Child changes everything
3. Nature is remade
4. Eden is rebuilt

CONCLUSION

Who is the Child lying in the manger? He is none other than the God-man who has taken on Himself our human nature, the one begotten of the Father from eternity and born of the Virgin Mary. Our Lord and Savior lies in the manger.

SERMON: WHO LIES IN THE MANGER? (ISAIAH 11:1–10)

Watch a sleeping newborn. The calm, deep breathing reveals a quiet and peaceful heart. This baby will have plenty of time to discover the trouble of this world, but for now there is no trouble, provided the child is loved and cared for well. As we look on a resting infant, the child's face often reflects the mother and father. The composed features of young children may tell us whom they favor. My two girls were blessed to receive the features of their mother.

Jesus had the features of His mother, Mary. Yet this does not tell us who He is. Jesus' physical appearance tells us only of His human heritage through David, though this is extremely important. Only God could tell us who the Child Jesus is. Our theme hymn states, "The little Lord Jesus laid down His sweet head" (*Lutheran Service Book*, 364:1). Dear God, tell us, who sleeps in the manger? What Child is this?

The Child lying in the manger is true God, begotten of the Father from eternity. Martin Luther's explanation to the Second Article of the Apostles' Creed confesses simply: "I believe that Jesus Christ, true God, begotten of the Father from eternity . . . is my Lord" (*Luther's Small Catechism*, 16). The Child in the manger is the Christ, who is God from God, begotten not made (Nicene Creed). He is begotten in such a way that His birth of the Father has neither beginning nor end, thus He is never more nor less than fully God, even as an infant in the manger. The apostle Paul tells us that this Child "was declared to be the Son of God in power according to the Spirit of holiness by His resurrection from the dead, Jesus Christ our Lord" (Romans 1:4). Only God can declare who this Child is to us. Without the Holy Spirit working through the Word to give us the knowledge, we could never know that this Child should be called the Son of the Most High (Luke 1:32; Augsburg Confession I). God's declaration tells us that the Child lying in the manger is God. And

13

this little Child shall lead us.

This Child, the Messiah, will judge with righteousness (Isaiah 11:4). But this statement sends a tremor of fear through sinful hearts. How will we stand in this judgment (Psalm 1:5)? This righteousness, however, is not the standard that shows wicked humans to be dying of the fatal wound caused by the fall into sin. The righteousness mentioned in Isaiah 11:4 is the gift of the Christ Child's own righteousness by which God counts us as holy in His presence for Christ's sake (Psalm 41:9). Because of the death and resurrection of Christ, God declares us poor sinners free from the burden of our sins. And God's declaring makes it so, even as He has declared this Jesus to be His Son. When God declares us righteous in His sight, we are righteous because of Christ. This Child lying in the manger says who we are.

The Child who lies in the manger will be faithful (Isaiah 11:5). From the broken garden of Genesis (and from eternity) the Lord planned to send the faithful Seed of Eve. "O LORD, You are my God; I will exalt You; I will praise Your name, for You have done wonderful things, plans formed of old, faithful and sure" (Isaiah 25:1). The little Child will be faithful where all the strength of man fails—and fails miserably. How embarrassing for us that where human might does not prevail, the weakness of the Child can and does.

The Son is faithful to His Father. The Child will reveal His Father's gracious will for poor sinners, and Jesus will lay down His sweet head on the pillow of suffering for which His Father sent Him. "When you have lifted up the Son of Man, then you will know that I am He, and that I do nothing on My own authority, but speak just as the Father taught Me" (John 8:28). Jesus is also faithful to us and to our need. Those who have been brought near to the mountain of Christ's Church will be fully protected by Him (Isaiah 11:9). Those who believe will be rescued from "every evil of body and soul" (*Luther's Small Catechism*, 22). God is faithful, and He will do it.

The Child lying in the manger is true man, born of the Virgin Mary. His human generation is by way of the house of Judah. Through His birth of Mary, the Christ is the Son of David according to the flesh (Romans 1:3). The Child lying in the manger has taken our flesh of a true human mother. His bones and sinews were knit together in her womb (Job 10:11), just as each of us was formed in our mother's womb. How weak the Christ Child appears, sleeping on His mother's breast.

According to His human nature, Jesus is but a shoot, a pliable branch coming forth from the stump of Jesse. He who is God from God is also man from man, conceived of Mary. Look upon the Child in the manger. Here is human glory cut down to size. The glory of God is humbled under the form of humanity. God has turned divine glory into human humility.

The Child puts His hand in the hole of the viper. He has power over the satanic snake. He throttles the enemy. The little Child in the manger can do it because this man is God. The Christ Child will, at the cross, crush the serpent's head.

The Child remakes nature—replacing enmity with peace and harmony. The ravenous beasts broken by the fall into sin are reconciled. They will neither rend nor tear again. The Christ Child leads all of nature to a new Eden. In this new Eden, the beasts again will live in harmony as they did with Adam and Eve before the first sin.

Who is the Child lying in the manger? He is none other than the God-man who has taken on Himself our human nature, the one begotten of the Father from eternity and born of the Virgin Mary. Our Lord and Savior lies in the manger.

Midweek 2

CHRIST'S SECOND COMING: FOR WHAT HAS HE COME?

ISAIAH 2:1–5

GOAL

That hearers would recognize and believe that Christ's first coming prepares us for His second coming in judgment.

TEXTUAL NOTES

See Luther's commentary, AE 16:27–33.

Isaiah 2:1

This verse represents the title of the coming section in Isaiah (chapters 2–4). The verses that follow are, of course, also in Micah 4:1–3 in almost identical words. The lack of a *waw* construction leads us to see this verse as a transition to a new revelation from God. Apparently, the speech that follows begins abruptly with that most pregnant word for the speech of the Lord, דָּבָר. God reveals Himself in ordinary human speech to the prophets, which the prophets then convey to the people of God. This introductory verse from Isaiah uses a common figure of speech in Hebrew—"the word that Isaiah *saw*"—this is similar to the English figure of speech: "I see what you are saying." In Isaiah (and the English as well), "seeing" is synonymous with perception that leads to understanding. The Lord's Word leads to understanding for the prophet and for his audience (see comment on Isaiah 2:2).

When commenting on this verse, Luther is especially interested in setting out the independent authority of the Word of God, whether those who deliver it believe it or not. God's Word comes to accomplish that for which God has sent it (Isaiah 55:10–11), often despite our human intentions. Luther writes: "The Word does not deceive. Works can deceive. The Holy Spirit accompanies the Word, though He may not be present in the preacher and in the hearers" (AE 16:27). God's Word never depends on the speaker or the hearer for its power and authority. The Spirit always accompanies the Word; Spirit and Word are never separate. "Judah and Jerusalem" are the seat of the King, to which both Israel and the nations will flow. Around this nexus the gathering crowds presage the final consummation of the age, because the Christ Himself comes to instruct in the Word. Perhaps this is the reason that the neighbor will have no need to teach his brother (Jeremiah 31:34).

Isaiah 2:2

"In the latter days" is more than just a prosaic reference to the end of time. This phrase refers poignantly to the messianic age in which the promises Isaiah is about to announce will come to be, with a view to their bringing about the ultimate consummation of the age. By telescoping the end (Matthew 24) with its cause—Christ—the latter days are drawn together in a single powerful image. This indeed is "seeing." The "mountain" (הַר) is nothing compared with the high mountains of the world. Its significance is not size but how the Lord uses it. This is the way of the cross, where small things are named with great names and are glorious to the eyes of faith. Luther identified this mountain as Moriah to connect it with Abraham's sacrifice of the substitute in the place of his son, Isaac (Genesis 22:2ff.). The "house of the LORD" refers to the temple and to the Church. This is the dwelling place of God. Here He comes to establish the Church on the mountain, so that it will attract all the nations. Isaiah was well aware of the insignificance of the land of Judah, given the ability of the Assyrian army to march across it at will (701 BC). He had experienced this, along with the miraculous salvation of God.

Isaiah 2:3

Isaiah allows us to overhear the conversation of those who have been attracted to Mount Zion where the Christ will teach. This international diplomacy is conducted by the King. His word of diplomacy is the Gospel. No wonder the nations will flow to hear His instruction. "Peoples" emphasizes the variety of persons—all are invited. "God of Jacob" is not merely a variation from the expected "God of Israel." Instead, it refers to the election by grace of God's people, an election settled in the primordial will of God and carried out in time in the patriarchal age. God gives to Jacob the name "Israel," and the reference here reminds us of sin and grace. The grace of God will be so compelling that even the Gentiles will flow to this place identified by the Gospel. "The church had to begin, namely, in a physical place, though the church itself is not physical. That mountain, He says, will be most highly praised, because from it the church receives its name and will be called Mt. Zion. Out of a physical mountain the prophet makes one that is spiritual and a kingdom that is spiritual. Therefore the church, or the kingdom of Christ, is an exalted mountain, the house of the Lord in a spiritual sense, because there it had its beginning in a physical way" (AE 16:28). At this mountain there is so much to be learned that everyone learns only a small amount, but even this small amount of knowledge is sufficient because it is the Lord's own Word. The Lord's promise is fulfilled at Zion on Pentecost when the Word of the Lord is poured out on all people and flows to all nations. And God's promise continues to be fulfilled. Even now as messengers continue to have breath to bring the Word of the Lord, His promises continue. Here תּוֹרָה and דְּבַר־יְהוָה are paralleled, supporting each other in their certainty.

Isaiah 2:4

The *waw* construction shows the advance of the messianic ministry and the fruit it produces. The attraction of divine judgment is that the Word judges the peoples to be free of their sin and guilt (Isaiah 11:4). No one would be attracted by nomistic judgment (Hebrews 12:20). The Lord's Word renders peace among those who previously slaughtered one another and made war against Zion. Therefore war becomes impossible. Before the age of professional armies, a conscript typically converted his household implements into weapons of war. Likewise, upon his return from battle, he would restore his army tools to their former peacetime use. Here, the Word of the Lord leads the peoples to convert their weapons permanently to more productive purposes. Micah adds the midrash of Micah 4:4 to emphasize the delightful tranquility of the Lord's ministry in the new age. Ultimately, the utensils of war can no longer be used because there is the peace of the Lord. The Lord provides the new universe in which human pessimism about war is overcome. "This is a war universe. War all the time. That is its nature. There may be other universes based on all sorts of other principles, but ours seems to be based on war and games" (William Burroughs, "The War Universe," *Grand Street* 37 [New York, 1992]).

Isaiah 2:5

"House of Jacob" is so identified to connect the people with their Savior (Isaiah 2:3). The logic here is a kind of moral greater to lesser:

"if the nations will later exhibit this longing for the Word of the Lord, should you not now, O Jacob, also walk in His light." Luther writes: "Therefore, O house of Jacob, to you above all this promise applies. Give thanks to God, do not disregard the light but 'while you have the light, believe in the light, etc.' (John 12:36), lest the darkness overtake you and you suffer harm" (AE 16:33). This is an attractive and kindly invitation to Jacob, as it was already described about all nations.

Sermon Outline

Introduction

In AD 43 the newly minted Emperor Claudius demanded an easy victory over the Celtic peoples of Britain to prove his mettle to a skeptical Roman people. Roman envoys did much to prepare the way for the Roman legions by developing friendly alliances with some of the British tribes. Diplomacy, however, did not turn swords into plowshares. The Romans spent three turbulent centuries trying to subdue the island and never fully succeeded. Human efforts never dulled the sword or turned spears into pruning hooks. Human wickedness always kept sharp the instruments of war.

Our warring madness can be cured only by the intervention of the Christ. Like alcoholics, human beings are drunk on the need for conquest and power over others. We need an intervention, and only Christ's coming will do. Into the bloodied mess of human existence comes One who will bring harmony among the nations. Christ comes to do what no human emperor or king ever could. He comes to bring peace.

I. The Word of the Lord Comes
    A. He comes to judge
        1. Through the Word
        2. Inscripturated
        3. Using shepherds to instruct
        4. On the Last Day
    B. He comes to bring peace
        1. He has led us in the way of peace
        2. He has defeated war
        3. In the end, instruments of war will become signs of peace

4. In the end, instruments of war will be agents of fruitfulness
5. In the end, war will be unlearned
6. In the end, all that will remain is the Light of the Lord

CONCLUSION

At the "Hot Gates," the Spartans fought with a calm tenacity, though eventually the Persians wiped them out to the last man. When Dienekes, a Spartan soldier, heard the battle would bring so many Persian arrows that they would blot out the sun, he responded, "So much the better, we shall fight in the shade."

When Christ returns, we will not fight in the shade, but we will live in the light of the Lord (Isaiah 2:5). He comes to bring peace.

SERMON: FOR WHAT HAS HE COME? (ISAIAH 2:1–5)

In AD 43 the newly minted Emperor Claudius demanded an easy victory over the Celtic peoples of Britain to prove his mettle to a skeptical Roman people. Roman envoys did much to prepare the way for the Roman legions by developing friendly alliances with some of the British tribes. Diplomacy, however, did not turn swords into plowshares. The Romans spent three turbulent centuries trying to subdue the island and never fully succeeded. Human efforts never dulled the sword or turned spears into pruning hooks. Human wickedness always kept sharp the instruments of war.

Our warring madness can be cured only by the intervention of the Christ. Like alcoholics, human beings are drunk on the need for conquest and power over others. We need an intervention, and only Christ's coming will do. Into the bloodied mess of human existence comes One who will bring harmony among the nations. Christ comes to do what no human emperor or king ever could. He comes to bring peace.

The Lord through His speaking brings judgment upon His people. His Law crushes human claims to righteousness. No greater burden could be placed on the human heart than to face the judging and powerful word of God's Law. When God speaks His Law against us, we have been marched forward into a pitched battle in which God is our adversary (Psalm 55:12). God challenges our works and status and slays us with the breath of His mouth. We are people undone. The Lord's promised coming includes a threat against us, because this God is the Lord of Hosts.

"Out of Zion shall go the law, and the word of the LORD from Jerusalem" (Isaiah 2:3).

Often Advent becomes merely pre-Christmas, a time to prepare to meet the Baby in the manger. Such preparation is foolish. We cannot prepare for an event that has already occurred. The first coming of the Messiah, the incarnation, enables us to look forward with joy to Christ's second coming in judgment. Because of Jesus' path from manger to cross to grave to resurrection, we can lift up our heads to see the kingdom of Christ coming to its fulfillment among us (Luke 21:28).

Jesus comes to judge all persons now, and this judgment begins with the household of God (1 Peter 4:17). Judgment falls on us every day and brings us suffering that blossoms forth in the fruit of repentance. Through the Word made flesh, God brings judgment to His people. This is not the retributive justice the world expects according to the Law. Instead, God graciously grants us favor in Christ, whose perfect life, suffering, and death satisfies God's demands for justice. Thus the psalmist said of God's justifying work, "[The LORD] will bring forth your righteousness as the light, and your justice as the noonday" (Psalm 37:6).

The Lord who comes to judge His children not guilty through the incarnate Christ continues to send this message of forgiveness in Christ through His speech written by holy men moved by the Holy Spirit. The Bible, though no less than a book, is so much more because the Lord's words are spirit and life (John 6:63).

The Lord will use His shepherds, His pastors, to instruct in the Word of God. He will send holy emissaries from Zion, proclaiming that our warfare has ended, our iniquity is pardoned, and that our Lord Christ has suffered for all sins that we might receive double forgiveness in return (Isaiah 40:2). Christ commissions men to speak for Him, telling us that in His first coming there is the Spirit and life that will stand at His second coming in judgment.

Christ's second coming on the Last Day holds no terror for us Christians because Christ's first coming in the incarnation tells us the meaning of His ultimate return. In these last days, through His speaking we will be vindicated, and there will be no more warfare between our God and us. Christ paid the ultimate price that we might have peace now and at the last.

Christ comes to bring peace with God, a peace that ever remains a gift of God. If it were up to us, we would ever be sharpening the instruments of war to turn them on God. Like a child who pitches a tantrum, we are on the warpath against our gracious God. And like a parent who holds tightly a child who is raging out of control, our God smothers our warring madness by enfolding us in the weakness of His body offered for us, wrestling us into the submission of faith as He did Jacob of old.

Christ leads us in the way of peace. He alone rescues those who desire to make war on God. He gives "light to those who sit in darkness and in the shadow of death, to guide our feet into the way of peace" (Luke 1:79). Not only has Christ defeated all our enemies of sin, death, and the devil, but He also has defeated war itself. Through the new testament of His body and blood, Christ declares all enmity between Himself and Adam's children to be over.

In the end, instruments of war will become signs of peace. After World War II, tons of naval scrap iron was converted into the raw material for cruise ships, skyscrapers, and automobiles. The U.S. economic engine melted the weapons of war and used the scrap for signs of peace and prosperity. The ultimate sign of warfare with God is the cross of Christ. God converted that which had been our weapon against His Son into the sign of our new life in Christ, who died in the fight to save us.

In the end, instruments of war will be agents of fruitfulness. Herman Melville wrote, "War being the greatest of evils, all its accessories necessarily partake of the same character" (Herman Melville, *Omoo*, vol. 2 of *The Writings of Herman Melville*, eds. Harrison Hayford, Hershel Parker, and G. Thomas Tanselle [1968]). When the Lord undoes war, He will undo the instruments of death too. The tree that brought death to Adam and plunged humanity into warring madness has become the tree of life. Eden's denuded tree has been plunged into the ground and watered by the blood of the only true Soldier of the cross. It has not been left barren, but now it has sprouted the life that provides fruit. Jesus promised, "Unless a grain of wheat falls into the earth and dies, it remains alone; but if it dies, it bears much fruit" (John 12:24).

In the end, war will be unlearned. When Christ comes again to harvest the fruit of His death, war will no longer be necessary. A new universe of peace will open before us war-wearied militants.

In the end, all that will remain is the light of the Lord. The movie *The 300* related the account of the Spartan's three-day defense against the Persians at the "Hot Gates." During this battle, three hundred crack troops stopped hundreds of thousands of Persians. This movie reveals the darkness that pervades the warring madness of man. Light comes only from the Lord, who lifts the smoking darkness of apocalypse and reveals the true life that comes to us in Christ.

At the "Hot Gates," the Spartans fought with a calm tenacity, though eventually the Persians wiped them out to the last man. When Dienekes, a Spartan soldier, heard the battle would bring so many Persian arrows that they would blot out the sun, he responded, "So much the better, we shall fight in the shade."

When Christ returns, we will not fight in the shade, but we will live in the light of the Lord (Isaiah 2:5). He comes to bring peace.

Midweek 3

CHRIST'S THIRD COMING: HOW HAS HE SAVED US?

ISAIAH 35:1–10

GOAL

That hearers would recognize and believe that Christ is the Lord who is continually coming among us through the means of grace to prepare us for His second coming on the Last Day.

TEXTUAL NOTES

See Luther's comments, AE 16: 299–306.

Isaiah 35:1–2

The region of the Arabah (עֲרָבָה) was well-known to the inhabitants of Jerusalem, because it lies to the east in the Jordan Valley. According to Isaiah's prophecy, this arid and inhospitable place would experience a shocking reversal. The desert lands would "shout for joy" (Isaiah 35:2 NIV). The figure of speech here is quite intense; after all, deserts do not make any sound. The mixed metaphor heightens the drama of the intervention of God, who accomplishes the impossible (Luke 18:27). But this shouting for joy, identified with the verb רָנַן, comes abruptly at the beginning of this section. And because it appears near the start, it sets the theme for the whole section. Such an attitude of joy certainly fits well with the quickly approaching Feast of the Nativity of Our Lord, now only days away. Isaiah 61:10 provides an interpretation of these words. The gap between appearances (current sorrow and suffering) and reality (joy in salvation—both now and in eternity) can be seen only by faith. "The church flourishes inwardly, not in power, in the

24

wisdom of the flesh, in the gleam of splendid works; but it walks along in a simple form, not in ostentatious holiness, and therefore appears to be quite forsaken and without any glitter. Yet there are internal flowers and delights there, but these are not visible, namely, confidence, peace, life, a cheerful conscience, things that are not seen" (AE 16:299). In contrast to typically parched and barren desert regions, Isaiah lists in these verses places that are celebrated for their fruitfulness: Lebanon (1 Kings 7:2; 2 Kings 19:23; Psalm 72:16); Carmel, which appears to have offered rich pastureland (Jeremiah 50:19); and Sharon (1 Chronicles 5:16; Song of Songs 2:1). Note in Isaiah 33:9 the contrasting irony as these same fruitful regions are identified as wasting away. The glory of the Lord identified in Isaiah 35:2 is none other than the coming of God in Christ. In the Old Testament, the glory of the Lord (כְּבוֹד־יהוה) was identified with the presence of God at His tabernacle (Exodus 16:10; 24:16; Psalm 104:31; Isaiah 4:5; 40:5; etc.), which was a theophany (see John 1:14) of the preincarnate Christ. Jesus Himself begins His ministry by going into the desert region (Luke 4:1). There He is fed on the Word of God alone. Note also "our God" often is used in connection with divine rescue and sacrifice.

Isaiah 35:3–4

The people of Israel knew what it was to be afraid. They had watched the Assyrians devastate the countryside and invade Jerusalem. Perhaps thousands perished in the countryside because the Assyrians were particularly efficient killers. Any soldier who has prepared for imminent battle knows about "weak hands" (see also Job 4:3) and "watery knees" (see also Ezekiel 7:17). This inordinate fear in the face of God's enemies is indicative of a feeble and weak faith. God calls on us not to be afraid because we have no reason to be fearful, for He brings victory over our enemies, even as He did in His perfect time over the Assyrians. When God commands us to stop being afraid, His words carry their own power to accomplish what He commands, for He Himself will come to accomplish salvation (Isaiah 35:4). But those whom God rescues often chafe at what they consider to be His tardiness. It is easy for those with anxious hearts to be dissatisfied with what may be to human understanding God's weak or tardy appearances of promised rescue. Some choose to believe they must save themselves. Luther tells us that patient waiting is part of faith: "God first permits people to condemn and persecute His church, as though He were absent, and then He will come very quickly" (AE 16:301). When God seems absent is precisely the time when God is nearest, because He is hidden under the suffering of the Church. God's salvation is worked by retribution and vengeance. This vengeance (נָקָם) is substitution—one act is paid for by another (Deuteronomy 32:35; Judges 16:28; Isaiah 61:2). The vengeance worked in the Messiah is a retributive justice in which Christ received the penalty while we receive the benefit.

Isaiah 35:5–7

In these verses, more impossibilities are attributed to God's rescue. Physical disabilities have long been seen as signs of human sin and our depraved nature. Only the Lord can remove the burdens of such disabilities. Notice it does not say that the disabilities will be no more, only that they will not weigh down (the blind *see*, the deaf *hear*; see Isaiah 35:5). The New Testament era is the time of fulfillment for this prophecy, and these are the signs of the messianic ministry (Matthew 11:4–5). Through the means of grace—Word and Sacraments—we who are deaf and blind to the things of God have all these burdens removed by the Messiah. The people of God are those who, though they did not physically see Jesus, "see" and who, though they did not physically hear Jesus, "hear." This is in direct contrast to the Jewish leaders of Jesus' day, who though physically "seeing they do not see, and hearing they do not hear" (Matthew 13:13). Another sign of the messianic age and ministry is abundance of life-giving water (John 7:38–39) in a land chronically afflicted with drought. Desolation has been overcome in Christ. Water also looms large in the life of the Church, who was brought through water to dry ground in Baptism. In Noah's time, water brought death. In Christ, water brings life (through Baptism) so that the world is made new through a drowning and rebirth in Christ, not because the world has been drowned in a flood. In the Jordan River, the "flood" swallows up the Son of God in His Baptism, and it is in the "ark" of our own Baptism into Christ that we are brought safely through the flood to God. During Noah's life, the flood cleansed the world of the sin of the many that God could give a new world to the few. At the remaking of the world at the Last Day, the One who died and in whose name we are washed gives eternal life to the many. The wicked were rightly put to death in the deluge of old. The Law discovered them and their evil. "The LORD saw that the wickedness of man was great in the earth, and that every intention of the thoughts of his heart was only evil continually" (Genesis 6:5). However, that inclination was not snuffed out in the cleansing of that first flood. Thus the Lord Himself underwent the cleansing flood of Baptism in the Jordan that in it there would be a death unto life in our own Baptism.

The new flood of our font now puts sin to death. John the Baptist began the reign of the Gospel at Jordan's bank, bringing righteousness that the Law could not bring. Water connected with God's Word brings life (Isaiah 48:21).

Isaiah 35:8–10

The commencement of the messianic ministry is connected with better roads and even with highways (Luke 3:4–6; Isaiah 40:3). Luther writes: "The Gospel has a wide road, a smoothed way by means of the completely firm Word in the footsteps of the holy patriarchs who have gone before. This is the royal and holy way" (AE 16:303–4). Isaiah may have in mind the road leading from the palace of the king to the temple. Ultimately, this road in Isaiah's prophecy points to the approach to God in the New Testament. Such an approach is direct and not made by human effort or works. Those cleansed by God through water and Word will be able to travel this road by the power of the Holy Spirit. It will be such an obvious path that even those who are prone to losing their way will not be able to blunder from it. The Word of God is perspicuous. In ancient times, lions roamed as far as present-day Asia Minor. To stumble on a ravenous beast in the lonely stretches of the Judean wilderness could be deadly to a traveler. No such danger exists on the Gospel road built by the Messiah. Luther writes: "They will walk safely and securely in freedom, because, redeemed by the Word, they cannot be led astray by laws and traditions, but walk in freedom of conscience. You know that Christian liberty is outwardly subject to all men but inwardly it is lord over all things. It can be condemned by no sin, Satan, Law, etc. Thus it has its being in Christ alone. Meanwhile let the outer man be subject to all, but let not the conscience give in on one tittle. You will say: 'However much I am an unclean sinner, sin, Satan, and Law have nothing against me. All these neither condemn nor confound me.' Thus no righteousness, uprightness, etc. will deliver us. Christ alone is our deliverer. This is Christian liberty" (AE 16:305). The "redeemed" are those who are bought back by the Lord. Their redemption is the result of God's vengeance and retribution. Isaiah 35:10 functions as an *inclusio* to bracket the material between vv. 1–10 (See notes on Isaiah 35:1.)

Sermon Outline

Introduction

Almost plaintively, the cradle hymn cries, "Be near me, Lord Jesus; I ask Thee to stay" (*Lutheran Service Book*, 364:3). How every Christian's heart burns with this desire! As we have heard repeatedly this Advent season, the Lord has heard our cry. Jesus became incarnate and lived among us: "We have seen His glory, glory as of the only Son from the Father, full of grace and truth" (John 1:18). And we know that He "will come with vengeance, with the recompense of God. He will come and save you" (Isaiah 35:4). He came once, born of Mary, and He has promised to come again to judge the world. But how does Jesus respond to our cry now, caught as we are between these two "comings"? Must we manage without His nearness now? Has Jesus left His Church without a head? Of course not. Jesus continues to come among us in the Word and Sacraments. There is no "best before" date on His promise to be with us always. The manger is never empty.

I. Scripture is the manger in which the Lord Jesus now comes

II. Means of grace
    A. Word
    B. Sacraments
        1. Holy water
        2. Holy blood
        3. Holy absolution
    C. Holy ministry
        1. Speaking to the anxious
        2. Strengthening the weak
    D. Remarkable results

III. Way of Holiness

IV. Ransom

Conclusion

Long before our asking, Jesus has determined to stay close by us forever. He has used the mundane means of Word and Sacraments so that between His first coming as the Babe of Bethlehem and His second coming on the Last Day there is still a coming of grace for us sinners. The manger is never empty.

Sermon: How Has He Saved Us? (Isaiah 35:1–10)

Almost plaintively, the cradle hymn cries, "Be near me, Lord Jesus; I ask Thee to stay" (*Lutheran Service Book*, 364:3). How every Christian's heart burns with this desire! As we have heard repeatedly this Advent season, the Lord has heard our cry. Jesus became incarnate and lived among us: "We have seen His glory, glory as of the only Son from the Father, full of grace and truth" (John 1:18). And we know that He "will come with vengeance, with the recompense of God. He will come and save you" (Isaiah 35:4). He came once, born of Mary, and He has promised to come again to judge the world. But how does Jesus respond to our cry now, caught as we are between these two "comings"? Must we manage without His nearness now? Has Jesus left His Church without a head? Of course not. Jesus continues to come among us in the Word and Sacraments. There is no "best before" date on His promise to be with us always. The manger is never empty.

Even as the children's Christmas service always includes a crude wooden manger—and always the same manger—so our Lord uses the familiar and seemingly crude means of speech and water and bread and wine to be among us. These means of grace have no outward beauty that should attract us to them. They, too, share the apparent weakness of the little Lord Jesus, "asleep on the hay." They, too, hide the Child, as did the clothes in which Mary, His mother, swaddled Him. But mundane words, water, wine, and bread are now employed by God to bear heavenly blessings to His people.

The Word of God bears God to us. Every time the manger of the Word is opened, it is a little Christmas as God comes to us. Our mouths are filthy hovels, yet God resides there through His Word. As we read and pray and preach Scripture, God comes through the Word. Martin Luther says of this coming: "It is in Scripture and nowhere else, that he permits himself to be found. He who despises Scripture and sets it aside, will never find him. We heard earlier that the angel gave a sign to the shepherds [Luke 2:12]; but to Mary or Joseph or to any other man, however pious they may have been, he gave no sign except the swaddling clothes in which he was wrapped, and the cradle into which he was laid, that is, the Scripture of the prophets and the law. In these he is enclosed, they possess him, they speak of him alone and witness to him and are his sure sign" (AE 52:171). Such a sense of weakness surrounds the Word of God that some among us choose to ignore, blaspheme, disregard, and ridicule it. Yet Christ places this Word in our hands, in our ears, on our lecterns, on our desks, and on our nightstands. But this Word is most powerful in our mouths and hearts, as St. Paul says, "The word is near you, in your mouth and in your heart (that is, the word of faith that we proclaim)" (Romans 10:8). If we have the inscripturated Word, that is the divine Logos (John 1:1) swaddled in the pages of Holy Scripture, we have the incarnate Word.

Young children often are frustrated by the limits of their immaturity. For example, they may be able to stand, but they cannot reach the refrigerator handle or have the strength to pull it open. This was a matter of great frustration to my daughters. They would stand before the refrigerator and bang on the door until they commanded an adult's attention. We adults understand children's frustration. We may satisfy a hungry child by taking the grapes from the refrigerator, cutting them in half, and placing the bowl on the table within our child's reach.

Our heavenly Father understands our spiritual need far better than we, His children, do. Through the Sacraments, God brings to us Christ, our salvation and our heavenly food. God puts the gift of life into the bowl of the font and on the table of our church, so to speak. We do not have to fly up to the divine pantry; God opens the larder and pours out His abundant gifts to us here, where we need them. When we cry, "Be near me, Lord Jesus," He responds, "Here I am in the Sacraments." Water combined with the powerful Word of God is applied to us through the apparently childish means of the washing of Baptism to cleanse us and wash away our sin. Wine and bread combined with the powerful Word of God are placed in our mouths for the forgiveness of sins. Cradled in our hands, placed in our mouths, this precious gift of Christ's body and blood now resides within us. He comes no closer than this, until He comes to rescue us from this present evil age (Galatians 1:4).

Sinners constantly need to hear the words of God giving us forgiveness. We need to hear these words often and personally, because in our weakness we doubt that God could truly be gracious to the likes of us. Our pastors use their filthy mouths cleansed from the altar to speak for God, "I forgive you." We cry for the Lord Jesus to stay, and He sends ministers from whom "we receive absolution, that is, forgiveness, from the pastor as from God Himself" (*Luther's Small Catechism*, 26). Be so near me, Lord Jesus!

When the Messiah comes, Isaiah says "the eyes of the blind [will] be opened and the ears of the deaf unstopped. Then will the lame leap like a deer, and the mute tongue shout for joy" (Isaiah 35:5–6). Who has ever heard of blind people who now see, those who are deaf who now hear, or the lame who now leap like the deer? Such things are signs of the new age that is to come. God speaks them into being. And at this new age, a way of holiness will be raised over the desert wastes. What was once an unfruitful land, a land consumed by sin and its rage, will become fruitful in the hands of the Christ. In His first coming, Jesus has paid the ransom to make us His people. Now we receive the fruits of this ransom through the means of grace, God's Word and Sacraments.

Long before our asking, Jesus has determined to stay close by us forever. He has used the mundane means of Word and Sacraments so that between His first coming as the Babe of Bethlehem and His second coming on the Last Day there is still a coming of grace for us sinners. The manger is never empty.

Christmas Eve / Christmas Day

Heaven in the Manger

ISAIAH 9:2–7

Goal

That hearers would recognize and believe that Christ is the Lord who is continually coming among us through the means of grace to prepare us for His second coming.

Textual Notes

Isaiah 9:2–3

Judah had suffered dark days. The Assyrians had worked much damage, slaughter, deforestation, and so on. The locustlike army hordes caused so much dust to rise in the air that the sun was shaded by the clouds. This shadow brought death. However, here Isaiah makes this shadow indicative of the cause of death: sin and human depravity. The Light, Jesus Christ, came to overcome this darkness. In Isaiah the verbs are clearly "prophetic perfects," which speak of the future with the certainty of the perfect tense. This prophecy is as good as accomplished for Isaiah. The "walk" in v. 1 is the continuous conduct of life (הַהֹלְכִים), so the New Testament uses καθήμενος, "dwelling" (Matthew 4:16), when quoting this verse. The people of God live this way continually, not merely when the Assyrians breeze into town for a little pillaging. This "great light" puts together the light of Genesis 1:3, the preincarnate Light of the world, with the adjective used in Genesis 1:16 with the incarnate lights or luminaries (הַמְּאֹרֹת הַגְּדֹלִים). It is significant that the One who calls Himself the Light of the world is also the One who, as the creating Word, first made un-incarnated light and that it is the first created thing. If creation is salvation, then there is at least a harmony between what is made and what is redeeming. This theme is hinted at primarily in the Johannine books, especially John 1:7–9. "People" here refers to all persons, both Jew and Gentile. Luther writes: "Here is pictured the fruit and power of this light which is propagated from day to day, not satisfied with the corner where the Jews live but spread abroad among the nations throughout the world" (AE 16:97). Matthew sees this fulfilled in the early Galilean ministry of Jesus (Matthew 4:15–16). The Light is salvation in its fullest sense. The sense of the divide between darkness and light is absolute here. There is no middle ground. There is only deep darkness or there is light. Light is God's gift; it is never a human achievement. Now those who rejoice address the One who brings prosperity. "Multiplied" in v. 3 refers to the expectation of plenty and prosperity that should occur because of the messianic ministry (Isaiah 54:1). Galilee, though prosperous at the time of Jesus' coming, did not share the full prosperity of freedom from sin that the Messiah would now bring. In freedom from sin is true prosperity. This expression of joy will occur in the presence of the Messiah (לְפָנֶי) (see Luke 2:10)—so the cradle song is right to sing of a wide awake Child who is not crying! Isaiah makes this joy synonymous with "joy at the harvest," a time of plenty and optimism, or the euphoric adrenalin-charged joy after a battle, when booty is divided and the combatants exult at cheating death.

Isaiah 9:4–5

Now Isaiah shares the reason for the joy of the previous verses. The rod and the yoke of v. 4 are indicative of hard service and are more appropriate to beasts of burden. God's people have become subjects of foreign rulers. Now the true King would liberate them. "His" in v. 4 is Israel, taken as a collective: "And in that day his burden will depart from your shoulder, and his yoke from your neck; and the yoke will be broken because of the fat" (Isaiah 10:27). Israel has suffered the earthly analogy to this at the hands of Pharaoh and now at the hands of the Assyrians (and later they would face it again at the hands of the Babylonians), but their slave burdens were only signs of a far worse captivity to sin. A "rod" can be a scepter or perhaps a mace, either of which would be indicative of authority to rule. Isaiah's reference to Midian in v. 4 connects God's plan to destroy the current enemies of His people with the devastatingly swift victory He brought to Gideon (see Judges 7–8). However, the people are warned that such a victory may be accomplished with similar weakness and apparent poverty of forces to show that God Himself is the victor. God's strength is made perfect in weakness, under the cross. Note, too, that Gideon's victory involves the sudden appearance of light in a dark place (Judges 7:16–21). There will be a decisive end to warfare in the work of the Messiah. How delightful this must have sounded to a people wearied by war. The words used in v. 5 for the implements of war include only the nonlethal sort. If even these are being destroyed, then certainly the deadly implements are equally unable to harm. The "boot" is essential to swift and sure marching. Unshod troops soon fall out of the column. Here the boot (סְאוֹן) is a *hapax*, which refers to the Assyrian marching boot, which made it possible to hear the Assyrian armies approaching from great distances. "Blood" points to the success of the soldiers. This is a real threat from powerful tyrants.

Isaiah 9:6–7

Now we learn the reason for the previous calls to be joyful at the defeat of the enemies. A Child, already introduced in Isaiah 7:14, is born. This seems implausible. No mere child could prevail against Assyrian troops, but this is the way of Gideon. The announcement of the Child (כִּי־יֶלֶד) comes at the beginning of the verse. Everything is focused on Him. He Himself will pacify the warriors (v. 5), no matter how implausible it sounds, so that there is peace for the people of God. Luther writes: "All these words are strong and intense. Above he spoke of the greatest affliction, of darkness and the shadow of death. Likewise of the Law, of sin, and of death, the most oppressive tyrants. Against them he now places the King born and given to us, who is to set us free from them and implant us into His peaceful and happy reign" (AE 16:100). "To us" (לָנוּ) is repeated in v. 6 for emphasis. The Child is born to the people of God. He is a public Child, given to us. He has set Himself to serve us. What this Child does is for us. He, though above all kings, is a servant, while all other kings serve themselves (see Matthew 20:28). This Child is "for us." Not just from His enthronement, but immediately from His birth the authority of the government stands upon His shoulders (Isaiah 22:22; Revelation 3:7).

This is no ordinary Child. The titles identified in v. 6 tell us who this Child is. Most commentators take the following attributes as four sets of two words. In the attribute "Wonderful Counselor," *wonder* is an abstract noun (פֶּלֶא), not an adjective. This Child is a wonder of a counselor. In Scripture, God is denominated the one who does wonder(s) (Exodus 15:11; Psalm 77:14; Isaiah 25:1). A counselor is a cabinet minister who offers advice to the king (2 Samuel 15:12). An "abundance of counselors" (Proverbs 11:14) is unnecessary for this Child who provides the wonder of counsel. He is wisdom incarnate. The attribute "Mighty God" is used only here and in Isaiah 10:21. The singular is used exclusively of the Lord. "Mighty" (גִּבּוֹר) is heroic. We have a God who acts heroically. He will certainly be victorious in His quest to serve us. Long before the New Testament, Isaiah sees quite clearly that this Child is also God, so he uses a unique compound: "Everlasting Father" (אֲבִיעַד). This Child will act like a father toward his children (Psalm 103:13). This is not a title of the *opera ad intra* (internal trinitarian relations), but an *opus ad extra*. The Child is eternally this sort of Messiah. Isaiah's final attribute is "Prince of Peace" (שַׂר־שָׁלוֹם). This prince can be a military commander or general (Genesis 21:22), a chief servant in the household of the king (Genesis 40:20), and the preincarnate Christ (Joshua 5:15). This compound appears nowhere else in the Old Testament. Especially interesting is the occasion when Moses is accused of being judge and prince (Exodus 2:14) and that this accusation is tantamount to an accusation of lèse-majesté. "Peace" is the ultimate desire of an embattled people, and this Prince will bring it to His people by His action. This peace is not piecemeal or temporary, but it comes complete and whole in the declaration of justification (Romans 5:1).

SERMON OUTLINE

INTRODUCTION

In Johnson County, Texas, a young boy in a Sunday School class was asked to name the place where Jesus was born. Blurting out all the ancient cities he knew, he guessed Athens, then Carthage. When he was told that the right answer was Palestine, he said, "I knew it was in East Texas somewhere." Perhaps the boy was not far from wrong. The Child born once in Bethlehem of Judea is not far from our congregation. He is closer to East Texas than we might think.

Jesus is not merely "away in a manger," but He is "here in our Church." As we have seen throughout Advent, the Church becomes the cradle in which Jesus condescends to be present. Christ, who is so little that He could be nestled at the breast of His mother, Mary, invites us to receive Him in His littleness on the lap of our mother the Church.[1]

---

1 He who is small enough to be present with His mother, Mary, may be presented to us by our earthly mother, the Church, because He condescends to be among us in the signs of preaching and sacraments. Even Luther makes the Church a mother and a bride in the same sentence: "Therefore Sarah, or Jerusalem, our free mother, is the church, the bride of Christ who gives birth to all" (AE 26:441).

Heaven is come down to the manger. And Christ's manger is here.

  I.   The Child is born
      A. Heaven has come down into the darkness
      B. A great light has been seen
      C. Joy is poured out
      D. The ancient oppression has been broken

  II.   The Son is given
      A. Wonderful Counselor
      B. Divine Wisdom
      C. Word given to us
      D. Wonderful fulfillment of the divine purpose
      E. Mighty God
          1. Child born (human nature)
          2. Son given (divine nature)
      F. Everlasting Father
          1. Compassionate
          2. Zealous for His children (Psalm 103:13)
      G. Prince of Peace
          1. Davidic prince (2 Samuel 7:12ff.)
          2. Redefines peace in His own person

CONCLUSION

In the reredos behind the high altar of the Lutheran Cathedral in Copenhagen, Denmark, stands Bertel Thorvaldsen's statue *Christus*. It beckons worshipers to "come closer." At Christmas the world heard God call, "Come closer." In the table set here, Christ calls, "Come closer." The Word invites us to the manger of the Church where Christ is laid. Be near us, Lord Jesus!

SERMON: HEAVEN IN THE MANGER (ISAIAH 9:2–7)

In Johnson County, Texas, a young boy in a Sunday School class was asked to name the place where Jesus was born. Blurting out all the ancient cities he knew, he guessed Athens, then Carthage. When he was told that the right answer was Palestine, he said, "I knew it was in East Texas somewhere." Perhaps the boy was not far from wrong. The Child born once in Bethlehem of Judea is not far from our congregation. He is closer to East Texas than we might think.

Jesus is not merely "away in a manger," but He is "here in our Church." As we have seen throughout Advent, the Church becomes the cradle in which the Lord Jesus condescends to be present. Christ, who is so little that He could be nestled at the breast of His mother, Mary, invites us to receive Him in His littleness on the lap of our mother the Church. Heaven is come down to the manger. And Christ's manger is here.

A child is born. How simply Isaiah puts it. A birth announcement is one of the simplest announcements we humans know how to make. What proud father does not say, "We have a baby!"

Mary had a baby. Heaven came down into the darkness. As simple as it is to say that a child is born, we must recognize who this particular Child is. This is God from God, as the Nicene Creed says (see also Isaiah 9:6). He is no ordinary child.

A great light has been seen. The Christ Child brings light where once there was only darkness. Those who walk in darkness walk in pain and suffering as they trip over obstacles and run into walls. People in darkness walk in ignorance of the path before them. Only light brings true wisdom, because it accompanies the One who is wisdom in the flesh—Christ, the great Light. Christ is not merely a great luminary, but He is the very source of light (compare Genesis 1:3 and 1:16). He provides light where there is nothing shining.

Some years ago, while visiting Siberia in the summer, a pastor was shocked to find the sun piercing his sleep at four in the morning. Like a laser beam, the sun cut into his fifth-story, east-facing, curtain-less room. That first day, he had no choice but to rise in homage to the new light that erupted in the Siberian summer sky.

When the true Light was born under the darkened sky, the stars were overwhelmed by the arrival of the true Light that "enlightens everyone" (John 1:9). Christ, the Light of the world, overcame the darkness and brought true joy. Because the Light came and abolished the darkness, joy has been poured out on the people who walked in the darkness.

In the birth of this Child, the ancient oppression has been broken. The victory of the Child is swift, shocking, and complete, just as in the day of Midian. In a battle that predated the Spartans at Thermopylae, Gideon's three hundred stunned the Midianites with a crushing defeat. Here the weakness of the few defeats the power of the many as "the LORD [gave] the host of Midian into your hand" (Judges 7:15). This same "weakness" clothes the Child born of Mary, but Jesus is strong to save His people from their sin.

The Son is given, but He is not merely handed over. He is given *to us*! In older editions of Martin Luther's commentary on this passage, printers often placed the words "to us" or "for us" in capital letters. They wanted to emphasize as boldly as they could that the work of Christ to save the world was not some abstract theological concept or philosophical idea. Christ was given not just generally, but TO US. How strange that the God who made us and who possesses us gave Himself *to us*, to sinners! Thus God acts *for us* by giving Himself *to us*.

We receive divine Wisdom through this Child. We receive this wisdom as we receive Him through the Word and Sacraments. The Word has been given to us, and in that giving the Word Incarnate gives Himself to us. Thus the baby born of the virgin in Bethlehem is ever reborn among us through the Word. The speaking of God in His Word conveys what it says. His speech does not merely tell us about Christ. It does not merely relate the lovely story of a child born in hapless circumstances so we may be delighted or filled with nostalgia. No, the Lord gives the story and speech and makes present to us what it says. God's Word is ever a creating Word, unlike human words or speech. We become overwhelmingly sure of God's presence here because He speaks His presence among us (Matthew 28:20); this is such wonderful fulfillment of the divine purpose to be a God for us. The sacramental action of this night's Eucharist is *for us*. From the "manger" of our altar, the Child serves us with His own body and blood for the forgiveness of sins.

Despite the ethereal optimism of the hymn when it says, "no crying He makes," we must confess that Jesus was a squalling child, suckling at His mother's breast. He needed His diapers changed just as we did. Mary's Child bears our nature, so we might bear His immortality. The Son given to Mary is God. Her Son is the Father's Son. The God-man dwells among us, "full of grace and truth" (John 1:14). Even the ancient witness of Isaiah is decisive about who the Messiah will be. By flesh He would be the son of David, but He also would be the Son of God.

Like a father is to his children, so our God in Christ is compassionate to those whom He has made and redeemed in blood. He is zealous for His children (Psalm 103:13). And His zeal brings God in Christ to live with us here as we draw near the cradle of His Word. The Prince of Peace comes from the house of David (2 Samuel 7:12ff.) and will occupy an eternal throne. Through Him peace is granted to those who know their sin. To them God says that because they are justified by faith in Christ, they have peace with Him (Romans 5:1). This peace is not wishful thinking or faint hope, as it is among humans. This peace is a reality that our Prince defines in His own person. Jesus is peace; therefore we have peace (John 14:27; 16:33).

In the reredos behind the high altar of the Lutheran Cathedral in Copenhagen, Denmark, stands Bertel Thorvaldsen's statue *Christus*. It beckons worshipers to "come closer." At Christmas the world heard God call, "Come closer." In the table set here, Christ calls, "Come closer." The Word invites us to the manger of the Church where Christ is laid. Be near us, Lord Jesus!

Children's
Messages

Midweek 1

WHO LIES IN THE MANGER?

MESSAGE

When I was a little boy, I looked forward to going to my grandparents' farm. How many of you have visited a farm (or live on one)? **Let children respond.**

To me nothing was better than helping my grandfather feed the animals—whether it was feeding chop to the hogs or hay to the cattle. When chores were done, Grandpa and I would make our way back to the house.

Once when I was about ten years old, I was coming back from doing chores and saw my grandmother waiting at the back door. Instead of a hug, Grandmother held her nose and chased me away.

"Grandma, why can't I come in?" I asked.

As she passed clean clothes out the door to me, she exclaimed, "You are not coming in here smelling like the pigs!"

I could not imagine why she thought I smelled like the pigs. Do you think I smelled like the pigs? **Pass around the overalls and let children respond.**

I returned to the barn, took a quick shower, and changed my clothes. When I asked my grandmother why I smelled so bad, she told me that the smell of the hogs goes into the clothes, which is why she wanted me to change my clothes before I came into the house.

Our sins make us smell just like the pigs. Although we do not always notice, our heavenly Father knows how badly we smell. And He tells us we smell too! But for us smelly people, God sent His Son, born in our world and laid in a manger. **Cradle the doll in your arms.** Our God is not afraid of the smell of our sin. Instead of chasing us out of His house, He came to our world. He wrapped Himself in our odor so that He could take it away from us. **Wrap the doll in the overalls, then place both behind your back. Sing stanza one of "Away in a Manger" with the children.**

VISUALS

• Small doll, to represent Baby Jesus

• Child's overalls, preferably exhibiting an unpleasant odor

READ

Isaiah 11:3b–4a: "[The LORD] shall not judge by what His eyes see, or decide disputes by what His ears hear, but with righteousness He shall judge the poor."

SING

Stanza 1, "Away in a Manger" (*Lutheran Service Book*, 364)

SUMMARY

Jesus came into our flesh to take away our sin.

41

Midweek 2

FOR WHAT HAS HE COME?

MESSAGE

As the children gather, grasp the closed Bible with obvious confidence. I need a volunteer to hold this Bible for me. **Help the child hold the Bible by crossing his/her arms over the book with the cover clearly visible. After the child has taken the book, say,** Now, (*name*), you need to get ready so that when I hand the Bible to you, you are ready to hold it. You need to be prepared so that when I hand the Bible to you, you don't drop it. **Continue in this manner until the children realize you are asking your helper to prepare to hold something he/she is already holding.**

Do you think I am being silly telling (*name*) how to do something *he/she* is already doing? **Let children respond.** I am foolish for telling *him/her* how to be ready to hold the Bible when *he/she* is already holding it.

Can we prepare for an event that has already happened? When was Jesus born? **Let children respond.** Yes, Jesus' birth happened long ago. Can we prepare for an event that happened yesterday or last year or two thousand years ago? **Let children respond.**

You are right. We cannot prepare for what happened yesterday or two thousand years ago. But we can prepare for what will happen tomorrow or in the future: Jesus has told us that He will come again. Should we prepare for that? **Let children respond.** How is (*name*) showing us how to prepare for the second coming of our Lord Jesus? **Let children respond.** Yes, (*name*) is holding on to God's Word. Jesus tells us, "Blessed . . . are those who hear the word of God and keep it!" (Luke 11:28). So at Advent we prepare for the second coming of Jesus by learning from God's Word about the first coming of Jesus. **Sing stanza one of "Away in a Manger" with the children.**

VISUAL

• A Bible of substantial size

READ

Isaiah 2:3b: "For out of Zion shall go the law, and the word of the LORD from Jerusalem."

SING

Stanza 1, "Away in a Manger" (*Lutheran Service Book*, 364)

SUMMARY

Much of Advent is twisted by our culture to become pre-Christmas. Through clinging to the Word of God, we prepare for the second coming of our Lord and Savior Jesus Christ.

Midweek 3

HOW HAS HE SAVED US?

MESSAGE

When my children were very young, they learned quite quickly where food could be found. When they were first able to walk, they would go there and pound on it until they got an adult's attention. Where do you think they went? *Let children respond.* That is right, they went to the refrigerator.

Our youngest daughter was particularly fond of grapes. She would stand at the refrigerator and pound on it, shouting, "Gapes, gapes!" It was frustrating to her when adults did not respond to her need. How many of you like grapes just like my daughter? *Let children respond.* If you would like some now from this bunch of fresh juicy grapes, see if you can reach them. *Hold the bunch out of the reach of the children.* You are never going to reach these grapes, no matter how hard you try.

Our sin and our weakness make it impossible to reach the food that God wants to use to feed us. Do you think God wants us to be hungry and frustrated? *Let children respond.* No, God wants to feed us just as I wanted to feed my daughter when she was hungry. So just like Jesus fed more than five thousand people or had a special meal with His disciples right before He died on the cross, He also gives us the Bible to keep us full of His Word and show us His love.

It is better when God comes down to our level and gives us what we need, isn't it? He does just what we can do with these grapes. *Lift the box from over the bowl of grape halves. Give children who want some several grape halves on a napkin. As the children return to their seats, ask the organist to play "Away in a Manger."*

VISUALS

• One bunch of fresh grapes

• Grapes cut in half, placed in bowl, enough so each child may have a few

• Napkins

• Cardboard box large enough to hide the bowl of grapes

READ

Isaiah 35:2b: "They shall see the glory of the LORD, the majesty of our God."

SUMMARY

The Lord's promise to be with us is continuously and abundantly fulfilled (Isaiah 35:4–7) through the messianic ministry of Jesus. And Jesus continues to be with us in the Church's ministry through the heavenly food He sends in His Word and Sacraments.

Christmas Eve / Christmas Day

HEAVEN IN THE MANGER

MESSAGE

Whose birth do we celebrate this *night/day*? *Let children respond.* How big are babies? *Let children respond.* What can they do after they are born? *Answers to highlight might include eat, sleep, mess their diapers, cry, nothing.* So babies do not do much that is useful.

Have you ever held a newborn baby? *Let children respond.* Were you afraid that you might hurt the baby? *Let children respond.* Do you think Baby Jesus was helpless like that baby you held? *Let children respond.* Yes, He was a helpless little baby.

You were probably born in a clean hospital. Where was Jesus born? *Let children respond.* Yes, in a stable, and it probably was smelly. Where do you sleep at night? *Let children respond.* Yes, you sleep in a warm bed, but Jesus did not have a bed. He slept in a manger, a box from which animals eat their hay.

Although Jesus was born in a stable and slept in a manger, the Bible tells us that He is called "Wonderful Counselor, Mighty God, Everlasting Father, Prince of Peace" (Isaiah 9:6). Do you know any babies who have names like these? *Let children respond.* Only God has special names like these. So who is this helpless, little, crying baby born in a stable and sleeping in a manger? Yes, it is Jesus, our Savior. *Read Luke 2. Conclude by singing stanza one of "Away in a Manger."*

VISUAL

None

READ

Luke 2:1–20

SING

Stanza 1, "Away in a Manger" (*Lutheran Service Book,*, 364)

SUMMARY

A children's sermon is redundant in the context of the reading from Luke 2. However, reinforce the full humanity of the God-man, Jesus Christ.

44

BIBLE
STUDIES

STUDENT

Midweek 1

WHO LIES IN THE MANGER?

ISAIAH 11:1–10

INTRODUCTION

Our Advent Bible studies focus on four texts from the prophet Isaiah that point forward to the coming of the Messiah. Isaiah's career spanned the years 740 to 680 before the birth of Christ. He prophesied to a people actively engaged in idolatry, adultery, and oppression—signs that they had forgotten God (compare with Deuteronomy 8:11). The powerful nation of Assyria served as God's messenger of judgment upon the kingdoms of Israel and Judah. As a true prophet, Isaiah called the people to repent—to face up to God's judgment on unbelievers, turn from their sins, and trust in God's gracious forgiveness and salvation.

QUESTIONS

1. This week we begin the season of Advent. The word *advent* means "a coming to" or "an arrival." List the three "advents" of Jesus—the ways that He has come, does come, and will come for us. Discuss how each "advent" is important to our Christian life.

2. The Lord sent Assyria to bring near-total destruction on Jerusalem in 701 BC. As a result of the slash-and-burn tactics of the Assyrians, many trees were turned to stumps. Yet Isaiah prophesied that the Lord would raise up the Messiah, "a shoot from the stump of Jesse . . . a branch from his roots" (Isaiah 11:1), who would restore His people.

According to Acts 13:22–23 and Revelation 22:16, who is this shoot, this root? Why might God have waited seven hundred years to fulfill His promise of the Messiah? Why does God sometimes delay sending help in our times of need?

3. "The Spirit of the LORD" would rest upon the Messiah (Isaiah 11:2). According to Matthew 3:16 and John 1:32, how did Jesus fulfill this prophecy? How would the Spirit assist Jesus' ministry? See Luke 4:17–19 and Hebrews 9:14.

4. In the Small Catechism, Martin Luther offers this explanation to the First Commandment: "We should fear, love, and trust in God above all things." Isaiah said the Messiah's delight would "be in the fear of the LORD" (11:3). In light of the First Commandment, what clue does this prophecy give that the Messiah would be no ordinary man? According to Luke 4:4, 8, 12, how did Jesus demonstrate perfect "fear, love, and trust in God"?

5. Isaiah 11:3–4 shows the Messiah has absolute knowledge and is absolutely just in His judgment of the poor and meek. How does the Messiah's justice differ from human justice? According to Matthew 5:3, 5, what verdict has Jesus rendered upon poor and meek Christians?

6. Isaiah prophesied that the Messiah's mouth would strike the earth and kill the wicked with His breath (Isaiah 11:4). According to Hebrews 4:12–13, what comes from the Messiah's mouth?

7. How does Isaiah 11:5 highlight the divine and human natures of the Messiah? How does Jesus personify this verse? See Matthew 3:15; 2 Corinthians 5:21; 1 Corinthians 1:30.

8. Read Isaiah 11:6–8 carefully. Visualize each image. Can you fathom this scene becoming reality in our present creation? Read Romans 8:18–25. When will this edenic scene finally happen?

9. In the paradise described in Isaiah 11:6–8, we are told "a little child shall lead them" (11:6). In light of 1 Corinthians 1:27–31, how is God's method of leadership different from the world's?

10. Read Isaiah 11:9. Describe how this prophecy has begun to be fulfilled in the holy Christian Church.

11. Isaiah says the Messiah is "the root of Jesse" (Isaiah 11:10). Read Romans 15:8–9, 12. For what purpose does Paul cite this passage from Isaiah?

12. The "root of Jesse . . . shall stand as a signal for the peoples" (Isaiah 11:10). How does Jesus fulfill this prophecy? See Numbers 21:8–9; John 3:14–15; John 12:32–33. How can we hold up Christ as a signal for the peoples?

CONCLUSION

Commenting on Isaiah 11:10, Martin Luther wrote, "When the prophets speak of Christ's reign, they speak of His humanity and of His godhead. The Root of Jesse points to the man. The fact that the nations seek Him shows that He is God" (Luther's Works 16:125). Praise be to You, O Christ!

<u>LEADER</u>

Midweek 1

WHO LIES IN THE MANGER?

ISAIAH 11:1–10

INTRODUCTION

Our Advent Bible studies focus on four texts from the prophet Isaiah that point forward to the coming of the Messiah. Isaiah's career spanned the years 740 to 680 before the birth of Christ. He prophesied to a people actively engaged in idolatry, adultery, and oppression—signs that they had forgotten God (compare with Deuteronomy 8:11). The powerful nation of Assyria served as God's messenger of judgment upon the kingdoms of Israel and Judah. As a true prophet, Isaiah called the people to repent—to face up to God's judgment on unbelievers, turn from their sins, and trust in God's gracious forgiveness and salvation.

QUESTIONS

1. Jesus' first advent occurred when He was conceived by the Holy Spirit and born of the Virgin Mary. After dying and rising to save us from our sins, He ascended to heaven, though He has not left us. Jesus is merely hidden from our sight in the Word and Sacraments, fulfilling His promise to be with the Church always (Matthew 28:20). In the preaching of the Gospel, in Baptism, and in the Lord's Supper (and in Absolution), Jesus still comes to deliver forgiveness of sin to us. Every Divine Service is a little Advent! Jesus' final advent will occur on the Last Day, when He will return *visibly* to judge the living and the dead. We prepare for

that coming by meditating on Christ's first coming and receiving His gracious presence among us through Word and Sacrament.

2. Acts 13:23 shows that Jesus is the promised "shoot from the stump of Jesse . . . a branch from his roots," Israel's Savior. Jesus Himself testifies to this in Revelation 22:16. After seven hundred years of waiting, many in Israel thought God had forgotten His promises. Yet from the remnant of Israel, God raised up Jesus as the Messiah. Just when hope appeared to be lost, God sprang into action to fulfill His promises. Martin Luther wrote, "It is certainly thus, that God does not help except in the greatest trouble and in the utmost need . . . so that it may be evident that the matter is managed by the hand of God, not by the plans of men. This is the Christian thing to do, to recognize the acceptable time and the day of salvation (cf. 2 Cor. 6:2), even when it seems to be a day of despair" (Luther's Works 16:118).

3. At His Baptism, the Holy Spirit descended on Jesus in the form of a dove (Matthew 3:16), and this dove remained on Him (John 1:32). Jesus was anointed with the Spirit to preach the Gospel, heal the sick, and inaugurate the year of the Lord's favor (Luke 4:17–19). Through the Spirit, Jesus made His perfect sacrifice to the Father on our behalf so that we who drink of His saving blood have our consciences cleansed to "serve the living God" (Hebrews 9:14).

4. The First Commandment reveals our utter sinfulness. From conception onward, none of us fears, loves, and trusts in God above all things. Yet the Messiah would delight in the fear of the Lord, something no sinner could do perfectly. When He was tempted by Satan, Jesus showed perfect fidelity toward His Father in our place. "We do not have a high priest who is unable to sympathize with our weaknesses, but one who in every respect has been tempted as we are, yet without sin" (Hebrews 4:15).

5. Human systems of justice often fail those with the least power, money, and influence, yet the Messiah judges the poor and meek rightly. Christians who are poor in spirit and meek are deemed "blessed" by Jesus, though the world cannot see their blessedness. Martin Luther writes: "The people of Christ's kingdom are the poor, the mean, the insignificant, the faint-hearted, the harassed, the lowly, the fearful. These He will judge; that is, He will make the just cause prevail, He will justify them, He will give them grace, He will forgive the sins of those

who acknowledge and confess them and do not rely on themselves. . . . The ungodly, who regard themselves as holy and defend their sins, are not of Christ's kingdom; they do not enjoy the righteousness and equity of Christ" (Luther's Works 16:121).

6. The Word of Christ cuts through all human defenses and reveals the sinful heart (Hebrews 4:12). Under the Messiah's judgment, we stand naked and must give an account for what we have done in our bodies (Hebrews 4:13). Luther says, "[The Word] smites and brings to naught earthly and ungodly men, toward repentance and toward conversion and toward constant enlargement of His reign" (Luther's Works 16:121–22). Yet the word of Law is not all we hear: "The rod is the spoken Word. Behold, lip and tongue and mouth of Christ are all who sincerely preach the Gospel" (Luther's Works 16:121). The word of Gospel has cleansed us in Baptism, which is the "washing of water with the word" (Ephesians 5:26). Jesus says, "Already you are clean because of the word that I have spoken to you" (John 15:3), that is, the word of absolution.

7. Isaiah portrays the Messiah as a man with a waist and loins, yet His belts are attributes that belong to God alone. Only God is truly righteous and faithful. Jesus personifies this verse because He is "true God, begotten of the Father from eternity, and also true man, born of the Virgin Mary" (Explanation of the Second Article of the Apostles' Creed). In the Jordan River, Jesus fulfilled all righteousness by undergoing a sinner's Baptism (Matthew 3:15), thereby standing in the place of all sinners under God's judgment upon sin. His Father made Jesus to be sin, though He was born without sin and never sinned. Thus we might become righteous in Christ (2 Corinthians 5:21). As Luther so aptly states, "We are dead in alien sin [that is, original sin inherited from Adam]; we must live by alien righteousness [that is, Christ's righteousness]" (Luther's Works 16:120). Because in Baptism we have "put on Christ" (Galatians 3:27), He has become our righteousness (1 Corinthians 1:30).

8. It is inconceivable that this present creation could become so peaceful. Paul describes the creation's frustration under God's punishment for sin (Romans 8:20–22). We feel this decay in our own bodies. Although we have already been adopted and redeemed through Baptism, we must look forward to the new creation God will bring about on the Last Day. In the meantime, we wait patiently through faith in Christ.

9. The leaders of this world rule by force. The Christ Child, upon

whom all the world depends, leads in humility and weakness. Advent and Christmas point us to the one true God, who turns everything upside down and inside out from what we would expect. Facing the Christ Child, how could we do anything but swallow our pride and boast in the Lord's goodness (1 Corinthians 1:31)?

10. When Christians receive God's forgiveness with gladness and begin to forgive others, when they delight in the peace of God and begin to abide in peace and love with one another, then we catch a glimpse of the ultimate peace that will exist in the Lord's new creation. Our privilege in the Church is to "be full of the knowledge of the LORD" (Isaiah 11:9), which brings about a renewed state of affairs. Luther writes: "The true knowledge of Christ begets harmony. . . . It is a cause of strife when everyone defends his own opinion. Those who know Christ forsake all human opinions, rely on the Word alone, and on the life and righteousness of Christ alone. In the world and in external affairs there is indeed inequality, but in Christ's kingdom all things are one. Laws cannot bring men into agreement. Faith in Christ creates unity and makes men equal, while every other kind of righteousness is condemned" (Luther's Works 16:123).

11. Isaiah 11:10 shows that not only Jews but also Gentiles will inquire of the Messiah and enter His resting place. Paul uses this passage, along with several other Old Testament citations, to demonstrate that Jesus as Messiah has shown mercy to Jew and Gentile alike.

12. Jesus said that at His crucifixion He would "draw all people" to Himself (John 12:32). That is, He would take the sin of all people into Himself and die for them so that all who believe in Him might live. Christ is the "serpent on a pole" (Numbers 21:8–9) to whom we may look for salvation from our sins and for eternal life (John 3:14–15). When we point others to Christ through His Word and encourage them to find salvation in Him alone, we hold Him up as a signal for the peoples.

CONCLUSION

Commenting on Isaiah 11:10, Martin Luther wrote, "When the prophets speak of Christ's reign, they speak of His humanity and of His godhead. The Root of Jesse points to the man. The fact that the nations seek Him shows that He is God" (Luther's Works 16:125). Praise be to You, O Christ!

Student

Midweek 2

For What Has He Come?

ISAIAH 2:1–5

Introduction

The primary alternating themes of Isaiah are God's judgment and His grace. Isaiah reveals that God's judgment will reduce proud, self-sufficient Israel to helplessness. God's Law still does this to us. On the other hand, Isaiah also reveals the gracious restoration of Israel in the age of the Messiah, the age in which we now live in the Church.

Questions

1. Who gave Isaiah the "word . . . concerning Judah and Jerusalem" (Isaiah 2:1)? What does 2 Peter 1:20–21 reveal about the Scriptures?

2. The "latter days" (Isaiah 2:2) run from Christ's incarnation to His visible return in judgment on the Last Day. Read Revelation 22:7, 12, 20. Why does "latter days" appropriately describe the time in which we live? In these latter days, what would Jesus have us do? See Matthew 24:42–44.

3. In ancient cultures, mountains often were associated with a particular god or were considered the dwelling place of the gods (for example, Mount Olympus). In contrast to this, Israel's God revealed Himself definitively on Mount Sinai with His personal name: *Yahweh* (usually rendered in English Bibles with small capital letters: Lord). Isaiah 2:2

says Mount Zion would someday tower over all other mountains. Read Psalm 2. When would Mount Zion be elevated? Who would reign from this mountain?

4. What events in the life and ministry of Jesus occurred on mountains? What might the prominence of mountains in His life symbolize?

5. According to Hebrews 12:22–24, how does the Church fulfill the prophecy concerning the "mountain of the house of the LORD" (Isaiah 2:2)?

6. According to 1 Kings 8:27–30, what was the importance of the "house of the LORD" on Mount Zion?

7. According to Isaiah 56:6–7, what was God's intention for the temple? What does Jesus say and do in Mark 11:15–17 to reveal that the Jews had not allowed the temple to fulfill God's intended purpose?

8. After Mount Zion is exalted, Isaiah says "all the nations shall flow to it" (Isaiah 2:2). What does Jesus do in Matthew 28:18–20 to ensure that this prophecy would be fulfilled?

9. Isaiah 2:3 speaks of people coming to the Lord's mountain. What section of the Small Catechism describes how we are brought to Mount Zion, the Christian Church?

10. Those who inhabit the mountain of the Lord will say to others, "Come . . ." According to Isaiah 2:3, what benefits await those who go up to the house of the Lord? How does the imagery of Isaiah 25:6–9 sweeten the invitation?

11. What part do we play in the fulfillment of Isaiah 2:3? What confidence does Revelation 5:13 give us concerning the ultimate fulfillment of this passage?

12. Isaiah 2:3 says, "Out of Zion shall go the law, and the word of the LORD from Jerusalem." In light of John 1:1, 14, to which "word of the LORD" does Isaiah refer? According to Hebrews 13:12, what would the Word go out of Jerusalem to do? According to Luke 24:46–47, how did Jesus arrange for His Word to go out of Jerusalem?

13. Isaiah 2:4 says the Word of the Lord "shall judge between the nations." According to John 5:22–24, what is Jesus' basis for judgment? According to John 12:47–48, what activity will be the basis for judging unbelievers on the Last Day? Why should believers look forward to Judgment Day? See 2 Timothy 4:8.

14. Isaiah 2:5 invites to us to "walk in the light of the LORD." According to John 8:12, how is this done? According to Psalm 119:105, where is the light found? What function do we who walk in the light perform for the Lord, according to 1 Peter 2:9? What moral result flows from the light, according to Ephesians 5:8–9?

CONCLUSION

Martin Luther wrote, "The Gospel is the force, power, and work of Christians, and those people are true Christians who from day to day learn the same Word more and more and do not quickly become disdainful and get sick of it" (Luther's Works 16:30).

LEADER

Midweek 2

FOR WHAT HAS HE COME?

ISAIAH 2:1–5

INTRODUCTION

The primary alternating themes of Isaiah are God's judgment and His grace. Isaiah reveals that God's judgment will reduce proud, self-sufficient Israel to helplessness. God's Law still does this to us. On the other hand, Isaiah also reveals the gracious restoration of Israel in the age of the Messiah, the age in which we now live in the Church.

QUESTIONS

1. Second Peter 1:20–21 demonstrates the divine inspiration of the Scriptures. Isaiah and his fellow prophets "were carried along by the Holy Spirit" when they wrote (2 Peter 1:21). God gave Isaiah the words to prophesy. His words, as well as the words of each biblical writer, are God's Word.

2. Revelation 22 emphasizes Jesus' promise: "I am coming soon!" The Christian response is, "Amen. Come, Lord Jesus!" (Revelation 22:20). Since we have been prepared for judgment because we have received the Lord's forgiveness of our sin, we can look forward to our Lord's return to judge us. Jesus bids us "stay awake" (Matthew 24:42–43) through repentance and the ongoing use of His Word and Sacraments, since He is coming "at an hour [we] do not expect" (Matthew 24:44).

3. The New Testament cites Psalm 2 (see Acts 4:25–26; 13:33; Hebrews 1:5; 5:5) to show that Jesus is the Son of God and the Messiah who would reign on Mount Zion. Christ is elevated in His resurrection above all competing gods and exposes their nothingness. False gods cannot bring life from death. Only Yahweh (the Lord) can do that.

4. The Sermon on the Mount (Matthew 5–7), the transfiguration (Matthew 17), the crucifixion (Matthew 27), and the Great Commission (Matthew 28:16–20) all occurred on mountains, which suggests Christ's authority as the great prophet (even as so many significant events occurred on mountains in Moses' lifetime; compare with Acts 3:22–23). These mountaintop experiences also link Jesus indelibly with "I AM," Yahweh (compare with Exodus 3:14; John 8:58).

5. Hebrews 12:23 literally says believers have come "to the [church] of the firstborn" (see the footnote in the ESV). The author of this Epistle shows that the Church is truly "Mount Zion," "the city of the living God" and "the heavenly Jerusalem." Christ exalted Mount Zion above all other mountains when He established the Church. When He sprinkles His saving blood on us in Baptism, Absolution, and the Lord's Supper, Christ lifts us to this mountain to dwell with Him forever.

6. Yahweh responded to Solomon's prayer in 1 Kings 8:27–30, saying, "I have heard your prayer and your plea, which you have made before Me. I have consecrated this house that you have built, by putting My name there forever. My eyes and My heart will be there for all time" (1 Kings 9:3). The temple in Jerusalem was the dwelling place of Yahweh on earth, as the tabernacle had been before it. Although God cannot be contained by heaven or earth (1 Kings 8:27), He chose to place His name in the temple as an access point for His people (1 Kings 8:28–29). There He listened to the prayers of His people and offered forgiveness of sins through the temple sacrifices (1 Kings 8:29–30).

7. Yahweh desired "foreigners" to be grafted into Israel through faith so they, too, could rejoice in the house of the Lord on Mount Zion. He said His "house shall be called a house of prayer for all peoples" (Isaiah 56:7). The Jews did not have missionary zeal and failed to fulfill God's purpose. Yet Jesus would purge the Jerusalem temple (Mark 11:15–17), and His own body would be the temple of the Christian Church to which people of all nations will stream.

8. Jesus commissioned His apostles to baptize and teach wherever they went, making disciples of all nations (Matthew 28:19). The mission of the Church continues today so that all nations flow to Mount Zion. Luther said, "The Gospel will be published among all nations, and some will be converted everywhere. . . . To [the church] the souls gather through faith; for when the Gospel is heard, hearts grow soft, rejoice, and come running" (Luther's Works 16:29).

9. In his Small Catechism, Luther's Explanation to the Third Article of the Apostles' Creed states: "I believe that I cannot by my own reason or strength believe in Jesus Christ, my Lord, or come to Him; but the Holy Spirit has called me by the Gospel, enlightened me with His gifts, sanctified and kept me in the true faith" (*Luther's Small Catechism*, 5).

10. The benefits of coming to the Church are infinitely valuable: "that [God] may teach us His ways" with the result "that we may walk in His paths" (Isaiah 2:3). Luther explains: "The ways of the Lord are His works, especially the works He does in us, namely, that He destroys the works of the devil, sin, death, sadness, fear, trembling, and all evils, then also our daily lapses; and He works the opposite in us: hope, righteousness, patience, joy, peace, etc. These are the ways of the Lord which His Word brings when it is heard and believed" (Luther's Works 16:31). Isaiah 25:6–9 portrays the eternal blessings of entering the Church, where the salvation of the Lord is found. Such an appealing glimpse of eternity with the Lord makes one wonder how anyone could refuse the blessed invitation extended by Christ to feast in His Kingdom that has no end.

11. As we saw in Isaiah 25:6–9, the Gospel invitation is so sweet that simply proclaiming its virtues will draw others to Mount Zion's feast. Our privilege is to invite others to worship so that they can be taught by God through Scripture and, we pray, come to walk in faith as baptized believers. Sadly, many refuse the Gospel call, refusing God's gracious teaching, "always learning and never able to arrive at a knowledge of the truth" (2 Timothy 3:7). Yet we have complete confidence that our Lord will succeed in drawing His chosen ones to Himself. Revelation 5:13 shows the consummation of all of God's work when not only people but also "every creature in heaven and on earth and under the earth and in the sea" will sing eternal praises to the Lamb of God.

12. "The Word was God. . . . And the Word became flesh and dwelt among us, and we have seen His glory, glory as of the only Son from the Father, full of grace and truth" (John 1:1, 14). The Word tabernacled

among us in the person of Jesus Christ so that He could be led out of Jerusalem to the cross to suffer "outside the [city] gate in order to sanctify the people through His own blood" (Hebrews 13:12). He sent the message of His saving death through His apostles, first to Jerusalem and then to the ends of the earth (Luke 24:46–47). Today the Word still goes out of Jerusalem, proclaiming repentance and forgiveness of sins in the name of Jesus.

13. The Word of God, Jesus Christ, has been given all judgment by His Father (John 5:22). Jesus says that whoever believes His words *already* has eternal life and will not come into condemning judgment (John 5:24). Since Jesus came that first Christmas to save, only those who reject Him and do not receive His Word will receive the judgment of condemnation when He comes again (John 12:47–48). Unbelievers actually condemn themselves because the Word has offered everything necessary for their salvation, yet they have chosen to reject Him. Believers, those who are declared righteous by the Word and trust Jesus, need not fear Judgment Day because the Lord Jesus, "the righteous judge," will award them the crown of eternal righteousness (2 Timothy 4:8). Luther wrote that God will judge "through the Word, He will convict many peoples, that is, everywhere in the world . . . so that they acknowledge that they are sinners and are condemned before God because they do not know God, do not fear Him, and do not believe Him" (Luther's Works 16:32).

14. Jesus, the Light of the world, freely offers the light of eternal life to His followers, those who trust in Him (John 8:12). We encounter the Light through the written, preached, and sacramental Word (Psalm 119:105). We now "proclaim the excellencies of Him who called [us] out of darkness into His marvelous light" (1 Peter 2:9)—that is, we speak and sing His praises in the Divine Service and tell of His grace to others. Since we "are light in the Lord" as we bask in the Light through Word and Sacrament, we cannot help but produce "the fruit of light" in our daily lives (Ephesians 5:8–9).

CONCLUSION

Martin Luther wrote, "The Gospel is the force, power, and work of Christians, and those people are true Christians who from day to day learn the same Word more and more and do not quickly become disdainful and get sick of it" (Luther's Works 16:30).

STUDENT

Midweek 3

HOW HAS HE SAVED US?

ISAIAH 35:1–10

INTRODUCTION

Isaiah 34 and Isaiah 35 offer contrasting prophecies about the future of Edom and Israel, respectively. Isaiah 34 reveals God's condemnation of nations who go their own way with no thought of Him. Such folly incites His anger (34:1–2) and brings His judgment upon Edom, who represents all ungodly nations (34:5). When God pours out His wrath (34:8), a wasteland results where once the land was fertile (34:9–17). On the other hand, Isaiah 35 reveals the love and mercy of God toward Zion, the future glory of the messianic kingdom, and the wisdom of trusting in God.

QUESTIONS

1. Isaiah 35:1–2 portrays a remarkable conversion of a country from barren to fruitful. What do Isaiah 55:10–13 and 32:15 identify as the causes of this profound change? In John 6:63, how does Jesus underscore the unity of these two causes?

2. Isaiah 35:2 compares "the glory of Lebanon" with "the glory of the LORD," and "the majesty of Carmel and Sharon" with "the majesty of our God." Lebanon was famous for majestic cedars. Mount Carmel and the plain of Sharon were known for lush vegetation. What do these expressions explain about the cause of the creation's joyful state in

Isaiah 35:1–10?

3. Isaiah 35:3–4 portrays Israel with hands drooping from fatigue, knees shaking, and hearts racing under pressure from ruthless nations. How, then, can Isaiah say, "Fear not!" to the people?

4. God's vengeance and recompense are instruments of salvation to deliver His people from fear (Isaiah 35:4). Battle must be undertaken. Blood must be shed. Suffering must be inflicted. According to Hebrews 2:14–15, who must suffer defeat so that we might be saved? What fear is removed from our hearts?

5. Isaiah 35:3–4 describes comfort that we cannot see or feel with our senses. When we peer into a casket, salvation from death seems a pie-in-the-sky promise. How does Jesus address our lingering fear of death in John 16:33? Although we possess victory in Christ, what does 1 Corinthians 15:26 say we continue to anticipate?

6. Isaiah 35:5–7 depicts the world after God's salvation has arrived. How did Jesus show by word and deed that Isaiah 35:5–6 was fulfilled in His ministry? See Matthew 11:2–6.

7. Israel is an arid land, so in the Bible water symbolizes life and salvation. How do Isaiah 44:3 and John 7:37–39 show the fulfillment of Isaiah 35:6–7? How do John 3:5 and Acts 2:38 demonstrate the ongoing significance of water among God's people?

8. The "way of holiness" is described in Isaiah 35:8. Holiness is an important theme in Isaiah. After reading Isaiah 6:1–7, describe God's holiness and the effect it has on people. What does the Lord command of and promise to Israel in Leviticus 20:26?

9. "The way" (Isaiah 35:8) is an important theme in the Bible. Who is the way in John 14:6? What or who is the way in Acts 9:1–2?

10. According to Hebrews 10:19–22, what is the way of holiness?

11. Isaiah says that on the way, "even if they are fools, they shall not go astray" (35:8). Why should this comfort us?

12. God's "redeemed shall walk" in perfect safety on the way (Isaiah 35:9) and "the ransomed of the LORD shall return" (Isaiah 35:10).

Describe our redemption and ransoming on the basis of Romans 3:23–25 and Matthew 20:28.

13. Isaiah says "sorrow and sighing shall flee away" (35:10). This has begun in the Church, yet we still experience sorrow and sighing. When will Isaiah 35:10 be completely fulfilled? See Revelation 21:4 and 1 John 3:2.

CONCLUSION

Luther wrote, "We have been redeemed and purchased at a great price, namely, with the blood of Christ. This is the thunderbolt against all our works. It has a passive significance. It means that we were all sold under sin and death. But we have been purchased by the Lord" (Luther's Works 16:305).

LEADER

Midweek 3

HOW HAS HE SAVED US?

ISAIAH 35:1–10

INTRODUCTION

Isaiah 34 and Isaiah 35 offer contrasting prophecies about the future of Edom and Israel, respectively. Isaiah 34 reveals God's condemnation of nations who go their own way with no thought of Him. Such folly incites His anger (34:1–2) and brings His judgment upon Edom, who represents all ungodly nations (34:5). When God pours out His wrath (34:8), a wasteland results where once the land was fertile (34:9–17). On the other hand, Isaiah 35 reveals the love and mercy of God toward Zion, the future glory of the messianic kingdom, and the wisdom of trusting in God.

QUESTIONS

1. The creative Word from the mouth of the Lord brings light out of darkness, life out of death, and fruitfulness out of barrenness (Isaiah 55:10–11). The Spirit accomplishes the same thing (Isaiah 32:15), because He is the very breath of God that gives life (Genesis 2:7; John 20:22). The Hebrew and Greek words translated as *Spirit* can also be translated as *wind* or *breath*, suggesting a fundamental unity between the Word of God and His Spirit. Jesus makes this explicit when He says, "The words that I have spoken to you are spirit and life" (John 6:63). This is why the Church recognizes the written Word of God as the Spirit's speaking and sees preaching as the Spirit's living voice sent to slay sinners with the

Law and give life through the Gospel. Likewise, when the spoken Word of God is combined with the elements of water, bread, and wine, the Spirit is there sacramentally to give us life.

2. The beauty of Lebanon, Mount Carmel, and Sharon is solely the result of God's creative work, just as He alone can reveal His glory and majesty to us. Yet humans, with their constant striving to be "like God" (see Genesis 3:5), delude themselves into thinking that this sinful world can be renewed by their own efforts. Programs that promote "world peace" or "saving the environment" are noble but unduly optimistic. Only God can make this sinful wilderness into a prosperous, fruitful land again. He begins this work in the Church, but only in the new creation will Isaiah 35:1–2 be completely fulfilled.

3. Isaiah 35:4 says the God of Israel will "come with vengeance, with the recompense of God. He will come and save you." Throughout Israel's history, God repeatedly rose up to punish their enemies and save them from destruction. Isaiah 36–39 recounts how God punished Assyria and inaugurated temporary prosperity for Judah under the reign of King Hezekiah. However, temporal salvation of Israel was never God's final goal. All Old Testament salvation pointed forward to the total salvation that Jesus would achieve for all humanity.

4. The Son of God entered the battlefield against sin, death, and the devil and fell in apparent defeat. Yet the devil could not keep Jesus in the grave. The Father raised His Son and thereby destroyed "the one who has the power of death, that is, the devil" (Hebrews 2:14). No longer can Satan function as the Grim Reaper. He can taunt us with death, but he cannot inflict it. Our Lord has freed us from that dark cloud that strikes terror into the hearts of all humans, that is, from death looming on the horizon. Apart from Christ, we are slaves to death, but in Christ, we have "passed from death to life" (John 5:24).

5. Jesus assures us that He has overcome the world, though we still face tribulation and death every day (John 16:33). Luther comments: "[The church] is pressed down by a very heavy cross . . . beset and harassed by a variety of internal evils, such as weakness of faith and falling into sin. Beyond all these, Satan, the tempter, fights against it" (Luther's Works 16:302). Yet in hope we await that day when "the last enemy to be destroyed is death" (1 Corinthians 15:26). On that day we will see and feel our salvation. In the meantime, faith must cling to the

Word and Sacraments of Christ in times of doubt.

6. The blind, deaf, mute, and barren were considered accursed. Their restoration to health and prosperity would signal the promised messianic age. Jesus comforted the imprisoned John the Baptist with the news that He was truly the Messiah as He reminded John's disciples of the witness of the healing of the blind, the lame, the leper, and the deaf; the raising of the dead; and the preaching the Gospel to the poor (Matthew 11:2–6). Miracles served to confirm Jesus' identity and the validity of the Early Church's preaching, but now that the Word of the Gospel is firmly established, the only signs we need are Word and Sacrament: "[Miraculous] signs . . . were necessary to confirm the new Word, signs that were added to the glory of the church, signs that are not done physically in the last time of the church, now that Christ is no longer weak. They were necessary then as a witness to the Jews, who ought to have recognized the church of God" (Luther's Works 16:302).

7. The Holy Spirit is often connected to water in the Bible. In Isaiah 44:3 the Spirit's outpouring brings into existence a well-watered paradise such as we see in Isaiah 35:6–7. Jesus connects the Spirit with "living water" in the believer in John 7:38–39. Significantly, the Spirit's coming is predicated on the glorification of Jesus—that is, upon His death on the cross and subsequent resurrection and exaltation. Afterward Jesus would send the Spirit at Pentecost. Water and Spirit work together for our salvation, as John 3:5 and Acts 2:38 show.

8. Since holiness is an attribute unique to God, it cannot be defined but only described, perhaps most effectively by observing the effect God's holiness has on those who encounter Him. Isaiah 6 shows how God's holiness terrifies sinful Isaiah, convincing him that he will die. Only God's forgiveness allows Isaiah to stand. In Leviticus 20:26, God promises Israel that the people will be holy to Him on account of His holiness. He desires the people for Himself so that He can shower His holiness upon them. Of course, this obligates the Israelites to live holy lives, but on the basis that God has made and will continue to make them holy by forgiving their sins and sharing His holiness with them.

9. Jesus is the only way to God (John 14:6). He reveals the truth of God to us and gives us eternal life as we follow His way in faith. The Early Church was known as "the Way" (Acts 9:1–2), perhaps reflecting Jesus' self-designation.

10. Hebrews 10:19–22 speaks of Jesus' sacrificial death on the cross and His sacramental bestowal of forgiveness and holiness to us. Since we have been washed clean in Baptism (Hebrews 10:22), we can "enter the holy places by the blood of Jesus, by the new and living way . . . His flesh" (Hebrews 10:19–20). In the true body and blood of Jesus in the Lord's Supper we enter heaven itself and participate in the holiness of our Lord.

11. We remain foolish sinners in this life, though forgiven ones. Even as we are ever both sinners and saints, the Lord will not let us go astray. He keeps us on the way through His Word, even if the world views us as fools for believing. Luther wrote: "The Word, too, is a word of foolishness. Therefore he says that those who are fools before the world but wise in faith walk on the way" (Luther's Works 16:304).

12. Romans 3:23–25 shows our need for redemption and how God has met our need by offering His Son on the cross to redeem and justify us, turning away God's wrath by spilling Christ's precious blood. The Son offered Himself as a ransom (Matthew 20:28) for all (compare with 2 Corinthians 5:15) so that He might serve us with forgiveness, life, and salvation. He has "redeemed me . . . purchased and won me . . . with His holy, precious blood and His innocent suffering and death" (*Luther's Small Catechism*, 5).

13. On the Last Day we will be set free from our sin and the effects of the sin of others. All sorrow and sighing shall flee away for good. Revelation 21:4 portrays our everlasting joy in heaven. First John 3:2 reminds us that we cannot perceive that we are God's children based on appearances, because "what we will be has not yet appeared; but we know that when He appears we shall be like Him, because we shall see Him as He is."

CONCLUSION

Luther wrote, "We have been redeemed and purchased at a great price, namely, with the blood of Christ. This is the thunderbolt against all our works. It has a passive significance. It means that we were all sold under sin and death. But we have been purchased by the Lord." (Luther's Works 16:305).

Christmas

HEAVEN IN THE MANGER

ISAIAH 9:2–7

INTRODUCTION

"The zeal of the LORD of hosts will do this" (Isaiah 9:7). Our Lord has such an intense desire to save us that He sends His only-begotten Son (John 3:16). Clearly God could save by force, but He elects to save by becoming incarnate as a child and going to the cross. Jesus has nothing to prove and saves us in the only way that could overcome enmity and establish friendship: He lays down His life for His enemies. He does not coerce us to follow but lovingly calls and invites us. O Christians, break out in song, for the Lord has come as a lowly babe to save us from our sins!

QUESTIONS

1. "Jesus is the reason for the season" sounds nice, but according to Isaiah 9:6 and Luke 2:10–11, who is the real "reason for the season"?

2. If Isaiah 9:2–7 were a nativity scene, Isaiah 9:6 would be its manger. This verse is the heart of this section of Scripture—indeed, of the Christmas season. This is the divine birth announcement of Jesus, true God and true man. What phrases in this verse highlight the Messiah's human nature? What phrases indicate His divine nature? How does Matthew 1:21–23 further reveal the mystery of the incarnation?

3. "The government shall be upon His shoulder" (Isaiah 9:6). How does Jesus fulfill this prophecy in Matthew 28:18?

4. "His name shall be called Wonderful Counselor" (Isaiah 9:6). The world sends counselors for marriage, grief, and guidance. These individuals can offer worldly wisdom, but not a single one is "wonderful." What wonderful counsel about Christ does St. Paul give us in 1 Corinthians 1:21–25?

5. "His name shall be called . . . Mighty God" (Isaiah 9:6). According to Deuteronomy 10:17, what is God like? Who is identified as God in 1 John 5:20?

6. "His name shall be called . . . Everlasting Father" (Isaiah 9:6). This title is surprising since the First Person of the Trinity is the Father. What is meant by "Father" in this title? See John 14:8–11, 18.

7. "His name shall be called . . . Prince of Peace" (Isaiah 9:6). How do Luke 2:14; Isaiah 53:5; and Romans 4:22–5:1 show Jesus as the Prince of Peace on Christmas, Good Friday, and Easter respectively?

8. How does Luke 1:32–33 present Jesus as the fulfillment of Isaiah 9:7? Compare those passages with Psalm 89:3–4 and 2 Samuel 7:11b–16.

9. Isaiah uses the past tense in 9:2–5, though the Messiah's arrival would not occur for seven hundred years. Because God had spoken that it would happen, it was as good as done. How does Luke 1:79 show the fulfillment of Isaiah 9:2?

10. Isaiah 9:3 says God has "multiplied" Israel and "increased its joy." What does Psalm 16:11 say is our only source of joy? How is this connected to Christmas?

11. The Assyrians placed heavy yokes upon captive nations, including great burdens on war-weary Judah. The breaking of that yoke would grant longed-for freedom. While Isaiah 9:4 prophesies in part concerning the removal of the Assyrian yoke, the ultimate fulfillment was found in Christ. How does Matthew 11:28–30 offer hope for those yoked by sin and guilt?

12. Isaiah says the Messiah's defeat of Israel's oppressors would be "as on the day of Midian" (9:4). Read Judges 7:19–22. How was Christ's victory over our foes like the day of Midian?

13. Isaiah 9:7 says the Messiah's reign will be established and upheld "with justice and with righteousness." According to Jeremiah 23:5–6, what will result from the justice and righteousness of the Messiah? According to 1 Corinthians 1:30, how does Jesus fulfill these prophecies?

CONCLUSION

Martin Luther wrote, "*Zeal* is love mixed with hatred, or angry love, or the anger of love. Therefore, while God loves us, He is angry with our enemies, sin, death, Satan, so that He can more abundantly practice His love toward us" (Luther's Works 16:102).

Christmas

HEAVEN IN THE MANGER

ISAIAH 9:2–7

INTRODUCTION

"The zeal of the LORD of hosts will do this" (Isaiah 9:7). Our Lord has such an intense desire to save us that He sends His only-begotten Son (John 3:16). Clearly God could save by force, but He elects to save by becoming incarnate as a child and going to the cross. Jesus has nothing to prove and saves us in the only way that could overcome enmity and establish friendship: He lays down His life for His enemies. He does not coerce us to follow but lovingly calls and invites us. O Christians, break out in song, for the Lord has come as a lowly babe to save us from our sins!

QUESTIONS

1. We are the reason for the season! "For *to us* a child is born, *to us* a son is given" (Isaiah 9:6, *emphasis added*). Likewise, in Luke 2:10–11, the angel said to the shepherds, "I bring *you* good news of a great joy that will be for *all the people*. For unto *you* is born this day in the city of David a Savior, who is Christ the Lord" (*emphasis added*). Jesus is God and needs no season for Himself. Yet we do need a season to hear the Lord's Word, receive His forgiveness, and be encouraged by all God has done for us through His Son.

2. The Messiah is described as a child who is born, which indicates

His humanity. The titles ascribed to Him and the fact that the government will be on His shoulder indicate His divine origin. In Matthew 1:21–23, Jesus' birth of Mary indicates His humanity, yet the evidence for His divinity is overwhelming: His virginal conception by the Holy Spirit, His name *Jesus* (which means "the Lord saves"), His title *Immanuel* (which means "God with us"), and the fact that He would save His people from their sins—something only God can do!

3. Jesus said, "All authority in heaven and on earth has been given to Me" (Matthew 28:18). The universe rests upon Christ's shoulder. Yet unlike an earthly ruler, Christ uses His authority strictly for the benefit of His subjects. Luther says, "In the kingdom of the world the prince or king alone is free, all others are servants. But in Christ's kingdom Christ alone is a servant, and we are free. . . . Thus in the kingdom of Christ those who serve rule, and those who rule serve" (Luther's Works 16:100).

4. The Wonderful Counselor reveals wisdom that is foolish to the world: weakness is strength, surrender is victory, death is life. It pleased God "through the folly of what we preach to save those who believe" (1 Corinthians 1:21). The message? "We preach Christ crucified . . . the power of God and the wisdom of God. For the foolishness of God is wiser than men, and the weakness of God is stronger than men" (1 Corinthians 1:23–25). Luther writes: "The kingdom of Christ is beyond grasp, reason, and experience. Here the flesh must be put to death with all its wisdom and judgment, and it must be grasped only by faith. We must believe that Christ's righteousness is ours. Reason wants to lean only on its own righteousness, not on someone else's. We *believe* life, glory, righteousness, and peace but on the contrary *feel* death, shame, sin, and trouble. . . . Lest we come short in the matter of faith He gives us counsel, that is, the Word, so that we may abide in so wonderful a government of His kingdom" (Luther's Works 16:100–101).

5. Deuteronomy 10:17 exalts the Lord above all other lords and gods and describes Him as "mighty" and "awesome." He is no needy god, but the one God we need. In 1 John 5:20, Jesus is called "the true God and eternal life," thus showing that the title "Mighty God" is appropriate for Him.

6. Luther writes: "*Everlasting Father* . . . indicates the work and business of this King, not His Person. This name fits no one else. He always

increases His reign, He always begets children and rules over them, He always remains the Father, He does not assume the role of tyrant, His children are always beloved. This is beyond question the most delightful kingdom" (Luther's Works 16:101). Jesus is the ideal Father who sacrifices Himself for His children. Further, in Jesus we see the face of the First Person of the Trinity, God the Father (John 14:10–11). Jesus says to His children, "I will not leave you as orphans; I will come to you" (John 14:18). In the Church, Christ feeds, clothes, and protects us, always keeping a room in the house prepared for each baptized child.

7. The song of the angels to the shepherds proclaimed that the Christ Child had brought peace to earth for those with whom God is pleased (Luke 2:14). God the Father wounded and crushed His Son for our sins so that we would not have to be wounded and crushed. Jesus took our place under the Law, being reckoned disobedient and receiving chastisement from God to achieve peace between God and us (Isaiah 53:5). Jesus was "raised for our justification" (Romans 4:25), and now that we are "justified by faith, we have peace with God through our Lord Jesus Christ" (Romans 5:1). Luther aptly writes, "The forgiveness of sins is justification, and peace follows justification" (Luther's Works 16:101).

8. Isaiah 9:7 says that the Child will have David's throne and an everlasting kingdom. Luke 1:32–33 says that Jesus will have the "throne of His father David" and His kingdom will never end. Psalm 89:3–4 and 2 Samuel 7:11b–16 are parallel prophecies of the One who would rule over the house of David forever, a prophecy fulfilled in Jesus. All these passages describe both the divine and human natures of Christ.

9. Luke 1:79 speaks of the purpose of Christ's coming: "to give light to those who sit in darkness and in the shadow of death." Luther writes, "The people of the whole world, Jews as well as Gentiles, were in darkness, that is, in error, unrighteousness, notions, a false understanding of the Law, etc. *Light* is the Gospel, the gift of the Holy Spirit" (Luther's Works 16:97). The darkness of our sin and rebellion cannot overwhelm the bright light of the Gospel, which scatters our guilt into oblivion as light scatters the darkness.

10. The psalmist prays to the Lord, "In Your presence there is fullness of joy" (16:11). As we receive Christ's gracious presence in His flesh and blood in our mouths this Christmas, we, too, have fullness of joy in the forgiveness of sins.

11. Christ's gracious invitation in Matthew 11:28–30 offers (oxymoronically!) an easy yoke and a light burden. Such things just do not exist in our world. As we come to Jesus and unload the yoke of sin and burden of guilt in the font, through confession and absolution, and on the altar, He places His righteousness upon us, giving us freedom from guilt and the Law. Thus liberated, we serve gladly under Jesus' gentle hand and rest quietly in the Gospel.

12. Midian sorely oppressed Israel. God called Gideon to "save Israel" and "strike the Midianites as one man" (Judges 6:15–16). Gideon rounded up thirty-two thousand soldiers, but the Lord told him to pare his forces back to three hundred. This was, humanly speaking, suicidal. Yet God commanded this so that Israel would know in no uncertain terms that He had given the victory (Judges 7:2). On "the day of Midian," the weak Israelites were handed victory without lifting a sword. Likewise, our victory over sin, death, and hell is achieved without any effort of our own. It was achieved in the weakness of the Christ, who also lifted no sword but surrendered in defeat upon the cross to save us. Although water, words, bread, and wine appear weak, humanly speaking, they convey the benefits of Christ's saving work to us now.

13. Jeremiah says that under the Messiah "Judah will be saved, and Israel will dwell securely. And this is the name by which He will be called: 'The Lord is our righteousness'" (Jeremiah 23:6). Paul says that Jesus Christ actually is our righteousness. That is, His righteousness covers our sin, so when God looks at us, He only sees the righteousness of Christ. The Messiah's journey to save us—from manger to cross to resurrection to ascension—reveals the righteousness of God "from faith for faith, as it is written, 'The righteous shall live by faith'" (Romans 1:17). Praise be to God for declaring us righteous in Christ Jesus!

CONCLUSION

Martin Luther wrote, "*Zeal* is love mixed with hatred, or angry love, or the anger of love. Therefore, while God loves us, He is angry with our enemies, sin, death, Satan, so that He can more abundantly practice His love toward us" (Luther's Works 16:102).

Worship
Resources

MIDWEEK VESPERS

(For use each week. See specific elements on pp. 77–84.)

HYMN

Stand

OPENING VERSICLES

PSALM

Sit

OFFICE HYMN: "Away in a Manger"
(Lutheran Service Book, 364)

READINGS

RESPONSORY FOR ADVENT

CATECHISM

SERMON

Stand

CANTICLE: Magnificat

Sit

OFFERING

Kneel/Stand

KYRIE

LORD'S PRAYER

COLLECTS

COLLECT OF THE DAY AND ADDITIONAL COLLECTS

COLLECT FOR PEACE

BENEDICAMUS AND BENEDICTION

HYMN TO DEPART

NOTES ON THE MIDWEEK VESPERS SERVICE FOR THE WORSHIP PLANNER

- This service follows Vespers in *Lutheran Service Book*.

- Depending on local custom and circumstances, the opening hymn and/or the Hymn to Depart may be omitted.

- The Psalm may be spoken or sung to a psalm tone. See pp. 77–83 for suggested psalm tones, psalm texts, and antiphons for each midweek service.

- The Office Hymn should remain "Away in a Manger" throughout the Advent series.

- It is suggested that the Magnificat be used as the Canticle.

- See choral music suggestions on pp. 77–84 and p. 96.

Specific Elements for the Midweek Services

Midweek 1:
Christ's First Coming: Who Lies in the Manger?

Opening Hymn: "O Light Whose Splendor" (*LSB* 891)

Psalm: Psalm 8

The antiphon is sung once by the choir and repeated by the congregation. The Psalm is chanted responsively (congregation chants verses in boldface). The antiphon (based on Isaiah 35:10; 11:6) is sung by all as indicated. A full score of the psalm tone and the antiphon (with flute descant) is available on the accompanying CD-ROM.

Janet Muth

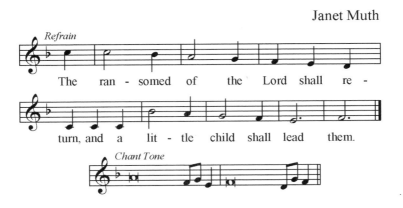

1 O Lord, our Lord, how majestic is your name in | all the earth!*
  You have set your glory above the | heavens.

2 Out of the mouth of babes and infants, you have established strength
   because | of your foes,*
   to still the enemy and the a- | venger.

Antiphon

3 When I look at your heavens, the work of your | fingers,*
   the moon and the stars, which you have | set in place,

4 what is man that you are mind- | ful of him,*
   and the son of man that you | care for him?

5 Yet you have made him a little lower than the heavenly | beings*
   and crowned him with glory and | honor.

Antiphon

6 You have given him dominion over the works | of your hands;*
   You have put all things under | his feet,

7 all sheep and | oxen,*
   and also the beasts | of the field,

8 the birds of the heavens, and the fish | of the sea,*
   whatever passes along the paths | of the seas.

9 O | Lord, our Lord,*
   how majestic is your name in | all the earth!

Glory be to the Father and | to the Son*
   and to the Holy | Spirit;
as it was in the be- | ginning,*
   is now, and will be forever. | Amen.

Antiphon

Readings:
Isaiah 11:1–10
Romans 1:1–6
John 1:1–18

Catechism (*LSB*, p. 322):
P.   I believe in Jesus Christ, God's only Son, our Lord, who was
        conceived by the Holy Spirit, born of the virgin Mary.

C.   I believe that Jesus Christ, true God, begotten of the Father

from eternity, and also true man, born of the virgin Mary, is my Lord.

Offering Anthem: "A Little Child Shall Lead Them" by Ralph Manuel (CPH 98-3844)

Collect:

Almighty God, our heavenly Father, because of Your tender love toward us sinners You have given us Your Son that, believing in Him, we might have everlasting life. Continue to grant us Your Holy Spirit that we may remain steadfast in this faith to the end and finally come to life everlasting; through Jesus Christ, our Lord. (*Lutheran Service Book: Altar Book*, p. 450)

Hymn to Depart: "Let the Earth Now Praise the Lord" (*LSB* 352)
"What Hope! An Eden Prophesied" (*LSB* 342)

MIDWEEK 2:
CHRIST'S SECOND COMING: FOR WHAT HAS HE COME?

Opening Hymn: "O Savior, Rend the Heavens Wide" (*LSB* 355)
"Come, Thou Long-Expected Jesus" (*LSB* 338)

Psalm: Psalm 2

The antiphon is sung once by the choir and repeated by the congregation. The Psalm is chanted responsively (congregation chants verses in boldface). The antiphon (based on Isaiah 35:10; 11:6) is sung by all as indicated. A full score of the psalm tone and the antiphon (with flute descant) is available on the accompanying CD-ROM.

Janet Muth

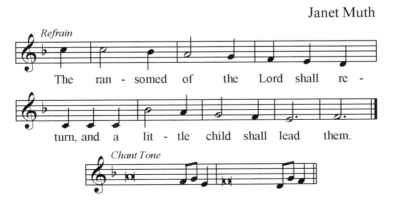

1 Why do the | nations rage*
and the peoples | plot in vain?

2 The kings of the earth set themselves, and the rulers take counsel to- |
gether,*
against the Lord and against his anointed, | saying,

3 "Let us burst their | bonds apart*
and cast away their | cords from us."

4 He who sits in the | heavens laughs;*
the Lord holds them in de- | rision.

Antiphon

5 Then he will speak to them | in his wrath,*
and terrify them in his fury, | saying,
6 "As for me, I have | set my King*
on Zion, my | holy hill."

7 I will tell of | the decree:*
the Lord said to me, "You are my Son; today I have
be- | gotten you.

8 Ask of me, and I will make the nations
your | heritage,*
and the ends of the earth your pos- | session.

9 You shall break them with a | rod of iron*
and dash them in pieces like a potter's | vessel."

Antiphon

10 Now therefore, O | kings, be wise;*
be warned, O rulers | of the earth.

11 Serve the | Lord with fear,*
and rejoice with | trembling.

12 Kiss the Son, lest he be angry, and you perish in the way, for his wrath is
quickly | kindled.*
Blessèd are all who take ref- | uge in him.

Glory be to the Father and | to the Son*
and to the Holy | Spirit;
as it was in the be- | ginning,*
is now, and will be forever. | Amen.

Antiphon

Readings:
Isaiah 2:1–5
1 Peter 1:3–12
Matthew 24:36–51

Catechism (*LSB*, pp. 322–23):

P.   Jesus Christ suffered under Pontius Pilate, was crucified, died and was buried. He descended into hell. On the third day He rose again from the dead.

C.   **He has redeemed me, a lost and condemned person, purchased and won me from all sins, from death, and from the power of the devil; not with gold or silver, but with His holy, precious blood and with His innocent suffering and death.**

Offering Anthem: "The King Shall Come When Morning Dawns" by Donald Busarow (CPH 98-2449)

Collects:

Almighty God, give us grace that we may cast away the works of darkness and put upon ourselves the armor of light now in the time of this mortal life in which Your Son, Jesus Christ, came to visit us in great humility, that in the Last Day, when He shall come again in glorious majesty to judge both the living and dead, we may rise to the life immortal; through Jesus Christ, our Lord. (*Lutheran Service Book: Altar Book*, p. 449)

Almighty God, You have called Your Church to witness that in Christ You have reconciled us to Yourself. Grant that by Your Holy Spirit we may proclaim the good news of Your salvation so that all who hear it may receive the gift of salvation; through Jesus Christ, our Lord. (*Lutheran Service Book: Altar Book*, p. 427)

Hymn to Depart: "Lo! He Comes with Clouds Descending" (*LSB* 336)

MIDWEEK 3:
CHRIST'S THIRD COMING: HOW HAS HE SAVED US?

Opening Hymn: "Hark the Glad Sound" (*LSB* 349)

Psalm: Psalm 111

The antiphon is sung once by the choir and repeated by the congregation. The Psalm is chanted responsively (congregation chants verses in boldface). The antiphon (based on Isaiah 35:10; 11:6) is sung by all as indicated. A full score of the psalm tone and the antiphon (with flute descant) is available on the accompanying CD-ROM.

Janet Muth

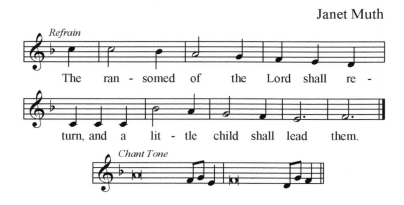

1 Praise the LORD! I will give thanks to the LORD with | my whole heart,*
in the company of the upright, in the congre- | gation.

2 Great are the works | of the Lord,*
studied by all who de- | light in them.

3 Full of splendor and majesty | is his work,*
and his righteousness endures for- | ever.

Antiphon

4 He has caused his wondrous works to be re- | membered;*
the Lord is gracious and | merciful.

5 He provides food for those who | fear him;
he remembers his covenant for- | ever.

6 He has shown his people the power | of his works,*
in giving them the inheritance of the | nations.

Antiphon

82

7 The works of his hands are faith- | ful and just;*
all his precepts are | trustworthy;

8 they are established forever and | ever,*
**to be performed with faithfulness
and up- | rightness.**

9 He sent redemption to his people; he has commanded his covenant for- |
ever.*
Holy and awesome | is his name!

10 The fear of the Lord is the beginning of wisdom; all those who practice it
have a good under- | standing.*
His praise endures for- | ever!

Glory be to the Father and | to the Son*
and to the Holy | Spirit;
as it was in the be- | ginning,*
is now, and will be forever. | Amen.

Antiphon

Readings:
Isaiah 35:1–10
Ephesians 2:1–22
Matthew 11:1–18

Catechism (*LSB*, p. 322–23):
P. Jesus Christ ascended into heaven and sits at the right hand of God
the Father Almighty. From thence He will come to judge the living
and the dead.

C. **That I may be His own and live under Him in His kingdom
and serve Him in everlasting righteousness, innocence,
and blessedness, just as He is risen from the dead, lives and
reigns to all eternity. This is most certainly true.**

Offering Anthem: "O Holy Child, Broken Heart" by Jon Vieker (CPH
98-3683)

Collects:

Lord Jesus Christ, giver and perfecter of our faith, we thank and
praise You for continuing among us the preaching of Your Gospel for

our instruction and edification. Send Your blessing upon the Word, which has been spoken to us, and by Your Holy Spirit increase our saving knowledge of You, that day by day we may be strengthened in the divine truth and remain steadfast in Your grace. Give us strength to fight the good fight and by faith to overcome all the temptations of Satan, the flesh, and the world so that we may finally receive the salvation of our souls; for You live and reign with the Father and the Holy Spirit, one God, now and forever. (*Lutheran Service Book: Altar Book*, p. 435)

Almighty God, grant that we, who have been redeemed from the old life of sin by our Baptism into the death and resurrection of Your Son, Jesus Christ, may be renewed by Your Holy Spirit to live in righteousness and true holiness; through Jesus Christ, our Lord. (*Lutheran Service Book: Altar Book*, p. 450)

O Lord, our God, in Holy Baptism You have called us to be Christians and granted us the remission of sins. Make us ready to receive the most holy body and blood of Christ for the forgiveness of all our sins, and grant us grateful hearts that we may give thanks to You, O Father, to Your Son, and to the Holy Spirit, one God, now and forever. (*Lutheran Service Book: Altar Book*, pp. 436–37)

Hymn to Depart: "Once He Came in Blessing" (*LSB* 333)

Christmas Eve

HEAVEN IN THE MANGER

EVENING PRAYER

Preservice music: "Away in a Manger" J. Muth
Stand

SERVICE OF LIGHT FOR CHRISTMAS EVE

L. The people who walked in darkness have seen a great light. *(Isaiah 9:2)*

C. The light shines in the darkness, and the darkness has not overcome it. *(John 1:5)*

L. Those who dwelt in a land of deep darkness, on them light has shined. *(Isaiah 9:2)*

C. We have seen His glory, glory as of the only Son from the Father. *(John 1:14)*

L. For to us a child is born, to us a son is given. *(Isaiah 9:6)*

C. In Him was life, and the life was the light of men. *(John 1:4)*

PHOS HILARON—HYMN OF LIGHT

THANKSGIVING FOR LIGHT

Sit

PSALM 141

COLLECT

ADDITIONAL PSALMS

OFFICE HYMN: "Away in a Manger" (*Lutheran Service Book* 364)

READING FROM HOLY SCRIPTURE: Isaiah 7:10–14

L: O Lord, have mercy on us.

C: Thanks be to God.

GRADUAL

Janet Muth

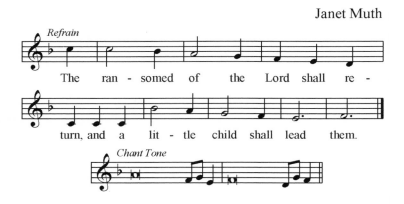

Antiphon (choir)

Men: To us a child is born, to us a son is | given;*
     And the government shall be upon his | shoulder,

Women: and his name shall be called Wonderful
     Counselor, | Mighty God,*
          Everlasting Father, | Prince of Peace. (*Isaiah 9:6*)

Choir: Sing to the LORD a | new song,*
     For he has done | marvelous things! (*Psalm 98:1*)

Antiphon (choir)

READING FROM HOLY SCRIPTURE: Matthew 1:18–25

L: In many and various ways, God has spoken to His people of old by
     the prophets.

C: But now in these last days, He has spoken to us by His Son.

SERMON

Stand

CANTICLE: Magnificat

Sit

OFFERING

Kneel/Stand

LITANY FOR CHRISTMASTIDE

L. Almighty God, heavenly Father, You have chosen to send Your only-begotten Son into the world, born of the virgin Mary, to be clothed in our human flesh, to redeem us from sin and death.

**C. Be near me, Lord Jesus, I ask Thee to stay
Close by me forever and love me, I pray.**

L. Forgive us that we have so often relegated Your coming to the stable of our concerns, preferring to focus on the hustle and bustle of life rather than focusing on receiving You in faith.

**C. Be near me, Lord Jesus, I ask Thee to stay
Close by me forever and love me, I pray.**

L. You laid down Your sweet head in humble circumstances while Bethlehem ignored Your birth. Grant mercy to all who humbly confess their sins, so that those who are humbled might be lifted up in Your presence.

**C. Be near me, Lord Jesus, I ask Thee to stay
Close by me forever and love me, I pray.**

L. You did not cry for Your own sake, but You wept over us with deep concern. Hold us to Your breast when we sorrow and weep over sin, that through Your love we might see Your joy through our suffering.

**C. Be near me, Lord Jesus, I ask Thee to stay
Close by me forever and love me, I pray.**

L. You have come near to Your people in the preaching of Your incarnation. Continue to grant such proclamation that gives life to Your people, though we have not deserved it.

**C. Be near me, Lord Jesus, I ask Thee to stay
Close by me forever and love me, I pray.**

L. Protect and prosper the preaching of the Gospel that creates and sustains faith. By Your means of grace place us with You, comforted and secure, on the lap of Mary.

**C. Be near me, Lord Jesus, I ask Thee to stay
Close by me forever and love me, I pray.**

L. Send Your Spirit to lead us back to the font that we might repent of our sins and receive Your healing power in Holy Absolution. Through our pastors, You have spoken gracious words of forgiveness to relieve us of the terrible burden of sin.

**C. Be near me, Lord Jesus, I ask Thee to stay
Close by me forever and love me, I pray.**

**C. Be near me, Lord Jesus, I ask Thee to stay
Close by me forever and love me, I pray.**

L. Lord Jesus, bless us all in Thy tender care, and take us to heaven to live with Thee there.

C. Amen.

The prayers then continue:

L. For the faithful who have gone before us and are with Christ, let us give thanks to the Lord:

C. Alleluia.

L. Help, save, comfort, and defend us, gracious Lord.

Silence for individual prayer may follow.

L. Rejoicing in the fellowship of all the saints, let us commend ourselves, one another, and our whole life to Christ, our Lord:

C. To You, O Lord.

COLLECT FOR PEACE

LORD'S PRAYER

BENEDICAMUS AND BENEDICTION

HYMN TO DEPART: "Silent Night"
(*Lutheran Service Book* 363; arr. J. Muth)

After the hymn is introduced by the handbells and flute, please join in singing as the handbells play.

Postlude

NOTES ON THE CHRISTMAS EVE
SERVICE OF EVENING PRAYER FOR THE WORSHIP PLANNER

- This service follows Evening Prayer in *Lutheran Service Book*.

- Depending on local custom and circumstances, an opening hymn may be included and/or the Hymn to Depart may be omitted.

- Additional psalms, should they be desired, could include Psalm 102 and Psalm 114.

- A full score of the Gradual psalm tone and the antiphon (with flute descant) is available on the accompanying CD-ROM.

- The Office Hymn should remain "Away in a Manger."

- It is suggested that the Magnificat be used as the Canticle.

- See choral music suggestions on p. 96. The arrangements in this service of "Away in a Manger" and "Silent Night" by J. Muth may be found on the accompanying CD-ROM.

Christmas Eve/Christmas Day
HEAVEN IN THE MANGER

DIVINE SERVICE

Preservice music: "Away in a Manger" J. Muth
Congregation stands and turns to face the processional cross.

ENTRANCE HYMN: "Break Forth, O Beauteous Heavenly Light"
(*Lutheran Service Book* 378)

INVOCATION

CONFESSION AND ABSOLUTION

INTROIT

L.   The people who walked in darkness have seen a great light. *(Isaiah 9:2)*

C.   **The light shines in the darkness, and the darkness has not overcome it.** *(John 1:5)*

L.   Those who dwelt in a land of deep darkness, on them light has shined. *(Isaiah 9:2)*

C.   **We have seen His glory, glory as of the only Son from the Father.** *(John 1:14)*

L.   For to us a child is born, to us a son is given. *(Isaiah 9:6)*

C.   **In Him was life, and the life was the light of men.** *(John 1:4)*

All: **Glory be to the Father and to the Son and to the Holy Spirit; as it was in the beginning, is now and will be forever. Amen.**

KYRIE

HYMN OF PRAISE: Gloria in Excelsis

SALUTATION AND COLLECT OF THE DAY

Sit

OLD TESTAMENT

GRADUAL

Janet Muth

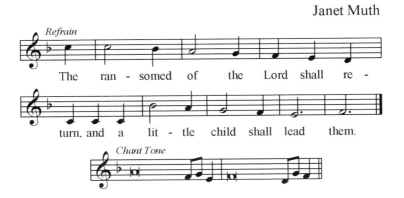

Antiphon (choir)

Men: To us a child is born, to us a son is | given;*
  And the government shall be upon his | shoulder,

Women: and his name shall be called Wonderful
  Counselor, | Mighty God,*
    Everlasting Father, | Prince of Peace. *(Isaiah 9:6)*

Choir: Sing to the LORD a | new song,*
  For he has done | marvelous things! *(Psalm 98:1)*

Antiphon (choir)

EPISTLE

Stand

ALLELUIA AND VERSE

HOLY GOSPEL

Sit

HYMN OF THE DAY: "Away in a Manger"
(*Lutheran Service Book* 364)

SERMON

Stand

NICENE CREED

LITANY FOR CHRISTMASTIDE

L. Almighty God, heavenly Father, You have chosen to send Your only-begotten Son into the world, born of the Virgin Mary, to be clothed in our human flesh, to redeem us from sin and death.

C. **Be near me, Lord Jesus, I ask Thee to stay**
Close by me forever and love me, I pray.

L. Forgive us that we have so often relegated Your coming to the stable of our concerns, preferring to focus on the hustle and bustle of life rather than to receive You in faith.

C. **Be near me, Lord Jesus, I ask Thee to stay**
Close by me forever and love me, I pray.

L. You laid down Your sweet head in humble circumstances while Bethlehem ignored Your birth. Grant mercy to all who humbly confess their sins, so that those who are humbled might be lifted up in Your presence.

C. **Be near me, Lord Jesus, I ask Thee to stay**
Close by me forever and love me, I pray.

L. You did not cry for Your own sake, but You wept over us with deep concern. Hold us to Your breast when we sorrow and weep over sin, that through Your love we might see Your joy through our suffering.

C. **Be near me, Lord Jesus, I ask Thee to stay**
Close by me forever and love me, I pray.

L.   You have come near to Your people in the preaching of Your incarnation. Continue to grant such proclamation that gives life to Your people, though we have not deserved it.

**C.   Be near me, Lord Jesus, I ask Thee to stay
       Close by me forever and love me, I pray.**

L.   Protect and prosper the preaching of the Gospel that creates and sustains faith. By Your means of grace place us with You, comforted and secure, on the lap of Mary.

**C.   Be near me, Lord Jesus, I ask Thee to stay
       Close by me forever and love me, I pray.**

L.   Send Your Spirit to lead us back to the font that we might repent of our sins and receive Your healing power in Holy Absolution. Through our pastors, You have spoken gracious words of forgiveness to relieve us of the terrible burden of sin.

**C.   Be near me, Lord Jesus, I ask Thee to stay
       Close by me forever and love me, I pray.**

L.   This *night/day* You offer Your body and blood to us poor sinners as the ultimate Christmas feast. You come among us as both Offerer and Offering at our altar. Grant that we might receive this feast in faith for the forgiveness of sins and the certainty of eternal salvation.

**C.   Be near me, Lord Jesus, I ask Thee to stay
       Close by me forever and love me, I pray.**

L.   Lord Jesus, bless us all in Thy tender care, and take us to heaven to live with Thee there.

C.   Amen.

Sit

OFFERING

Stand

OFFERTORY

PREFACE

SANCTUS

PRAYER OF THANKSGIVING

LORD'S PRAYER

THE WORDS OF OUR LORD

PAX DOMINI

AGNUS DEI

Sit

DISTRIBUTION HYMN(S)

"Lo, How a Rose E'er Blooming" (*Lutheran Service Book* 359)

"Once in Royal David's City" (*Lutheran Service Book* 376)

"Where Shepherds Lately Knelt" (*Lutheran Service Book* 369)

(Additional hymns or choral music, especially the anthem "Of the Father's Love Begotten" [arr. J. Muth], may be included according to local custom.)

Stand

NUNC DIMITTIS

POST-COMMUNION COLLECT

BENEDICTION

HYMN TO DEPART: "Silent Night"
(*Lutheran Service Book* 363; arr. J. Muth)

After the hymn is introduced by the handbells and flute, please join in singing as the handbells play.

Postlude

NOTES ON THE CHRISTMAS EVE / CHRISTMAS DAY DIVINE SERVICE FOR THE WORSHIP PLANNER

- This service follows Setting One of the Divine Service in *Lutheran Service Book*.

- Depending on local custom and circumstances, an opening hymn may be included and/or the Hymn to Depart may be omitted.

- Old Testament Reading:
  Christmas Eve: Isaiah 7:10–14
  Christmas Day: Isaiah 52:7–10

- A full score of the Gradual psalm tone and the antiphon (with flute descant) is available on the accompanying CD-ROM.

- Epistle:
  Christmas Eve: 1 John 4:7–16
  Christmas Day: Hebrews 1:1–6 (7–12)

- Holy Gospel:
  Christmas Eve: Matthew 1:18–25
  Christmas Day: John 1:1–14 (15–18)

- The Hymn of the Day should remain "Away in a Manger."

- See choral music suggestions on p. 96. The arrangements in this service of "Away in a Manger," "Of the Father's Love Begotten," and "Silent Night" by J. Muth may be found on the accompanying CD-ROM.

CHORAL AND INSTRUMENTAL MUSIC

TITLE	VOICING/ INSTRUMENTATION	COMPOSER/ ARRANGER	VENDOR & STOCK NO.
Away in a Manger	Children, flute, handbells	Janet Muth	on accompanying CD-ROM
Away in a Manger	2 pt mixed, piano, opt. flute or C instrument	Jantz Black	Augsburg Fortress 9780800623883
Away in a Manger	SATB, violin, keyboard	Walter Pelz	Augsburg Fortress 9780800646066
Antiphon	Congregation, organ, opt. flute descant	Janet Muth	on accompanying CD-ROM
Psalm tone	Congregation, organ	Henry Gerike	*Lutheran Service Book*; on accompanying CD-ROM
A Little Child Shall Lead Them	SATB	Ralph Manuel	CPH 98-3844
The King Shall Come When Morning Dawns	SAB	Donald Busarow	CPH 98-2449
O Holy Child, Broken Heart	SAB	Jon Vieker	CPH 98-3683
I Believe in One God	Mixed voices, alto or bass-baritone solo	Richard Wegner	MorningStar 80-850
Lo! He Comes with Clouds Descending	Choral descant	Jonathan A. Kohrs	CPH 97-6718 (in Hymnal Supplement 98: Vocal Descants)
Lo! He Comes with Clouds Descending	Handbell descant	John A. Behnke	CPH 97-6720 (in Hymnal Supplement 98: Handbell Descants)
Lo! He Comes with Clouds Descending	Instrumental descant	Donald Busarow	CPH 97-6719 (in Hymnal Supplement 98: Instrumental Descants)
O Light Whose Splendor	Instrumental descant	Donald Busarow	CPH 97-6719 (in Hymnal Supplement 98: Instrumental Descants)